Stadium Stories:

Penn State Nittany Lions

Stadium Stories™ Series

Stadium Stories:

Penn State Nittany Lions

Colorful Tales of the Blue and White

Rich Scarcella

The Globe Pequot Press

GUILFORD, CONNECTICUT

Stadium Stories is a trademark of Morris Book Publishing, LLC.

Text design: Casey Shain
All photos are courtesy of Penn State University Photographics, except where otherwise noted.

Library of Congress Cataloging-in-Publication Data
Scarcella, Rich.
    Stadium Stories : Penn State Nittany Lions : colorful tales of the blue and white / Rich Scarcella. — 1st ed.
        p. cm. — (Stadium stories series)
    ISBN 0-7627-2760-8
        1. Pennsylvania State University—Football—Anecdotes.
2. Penn State Nittany Lions (Football team)—Anecdotes.
I. Title. II. Series.

 GV958.P46S33 2003
 796.332'63'09748—dc22   2003061792

Manufactured in the United States of America
First Edition/First Printing

Contents

Acknowledgments

My thanks go to Penn State assistant athletic director Jeff Nelson, assistant sports information director Brian Siegrist, and the rest of their staff for their invaluable help; Lou Prato, author of the *Penn State Football Encyclopedia*, whose book provided a great research tool; and the dozens of former Penn State players who allowed me to interview them. A special thanks goes to my wife, Sandy, who provided encouragement and support throughout the project.

Legacy of Excellence

J im Tarman, the former Penn State athletic director, and his wife were on a Civil War tour in 2000 and found themselves in a tiny drugstore in Vicksburg, Mississippi. A woman was working behind the counter in a turn-of-the-century store when she noticed Tarman's name tag. "She looked at my name tag and it said, 'State College,'" Tarman said. "She turned to me and asked, 'How long is Joe going to coach?' This was in Vicksburg, Mississippi."

Joe Paterno has heard that question and answered it more than any other in the last twenty years. He first said in the mid-1980s that he would coach "another four or five years" and repeated that answer several times through the 1990s. So, when the seventy-six-year-old Paterno said a few weeks after the 2002 season ended that he would coach until 2006 and reassess his feelings then, most people yawned. The ageless Paterno might be eighty then, but they have no reason to doubt that he will still be coaching.

Paterno's critics howled in 2000 and 2001 when Penn State posted back-to-back losing seasons for the first time since 1931 and 1932—when Paterno was six years old. They suggested that the game had passed him by and that he could not relate to his players, the same criticism he has heard for years.

But after the Nittany Lions started the 2001 season 0–4, they won fourteen of their next twenty-one games, gave Paterno his record 324th victory, and finished in the top fifteen in the nation in 2002 with a 9–4 record.

"I like coaching," Paterno said. "I enjoy it. There's nothing I'd rather do. As long as I feel healthy enough to do it and coach the way I want to coach, I never want to be the guy up in the tower. I want to get involved with the players and do active coaching on the field. If I don't do a good job, I'll change my mind."

Since arriving at Penn State as an assistant coach in 1950, Joe Paterno has been coach, teacher, father figure, benefactor, and icon. He ranks as the all-time leader in major college football wins with 336 entering the 2003 season and owns two national championships and five perfect seasons.

He's built a framework at Penn State, where football players are legitimate student-athletes and graduate. Somebody coined it "The Grand Experiment." He has taught his players lessons beyond football. Twenty-four of his players have been named Academic All-Americans, including center Joe Iorio in 2002. Fourteen of them have been named Hall of Fame scholar-athletes.

"No one had as much impact on my life as Joe," said Jack Ham, the legendary Penn State and Pittsburgh Steeler linebacker, who asked Paterno to present him when he was inducted into the Pro Football Hall of Fame. "He made sure football wasn't the most important thing. He was adamant about getting your degree.

"He put football in perspective. He instilled in me that football was just like any extracurricular activity. I think I was very, very fortunate to play for him."

And Paterno puts his beliefs to work in other ways. When the toddler son of one of his former players was diagnosed with a brain tumor, it was Paterno who behind the scenes directed large sums of money into a medical fund.

Joe Paterno has posted a record 336 wins in thirty-seven seasons as the head coach at Penn State and has coached twenty-four Academic All-Americans.

As benefactor, he and his wife, Sue, headed a campaign that raised $14 million for a new wing to the campus library. A few years later, they donated $3.5 million to expand the library, endow faculty positions and scholarships, and support the building of a new spiritual center. He also has lent his name to two Penn State academic campaigns in the last twenty years that have raised more than $1.6 billion.

"The library doesn't have an alumni group, like the individual colleges and schools at Penn State," Paterno explained. "It's like a little orphan. To use the good things we've received from athletics toward the library helps set a good tone for everybody. . . . We in athletics should realize that we have a responsibility to academics."

Although Joe Paterno and Penn State are interchangeable, the marriage almost didn't happen. Rip Engle, his coach at Brown, left Rhode Island after Paterno's senior year to take the job at Penn State. Engle retained several Lions assistant coaches and had one opening, which he offered to his former quarterback.

Paterno was planning to follow in his father's footsteps and attend Boston University Law School. Angelo Paterno had gone to law school at night and became a lawyer while in his forties. But when Engle called, Paterno told his father that he wanted to put law school on hold and take a shot at coaching.

His father told him to be the best coach he can be. The guy from Brooklyn, New York, who intended to stay in central Pennsylvania for a little while, has stretched that stay to more than fifty years. "Anybody who thinks they're going to be able to stay in one place as long as I've been [here] or stay in coaching as long as I've been is a real optimist," Paterno said. "But it's been fun. It's been enjoyable. I've had good health. I

Joe Paterno established Penn State as a national power after succeeding Rip Engle as head coach in 1966.

got good genes from my parents. I married a wonderful woman who has made it possible for me to do it."

Paterno served on Engle's staff and eventually became his right-hand man. During the sixteen seasons that he was on Engle's staff, he married the former Suzanne Pohland, turned down overtures from Yale officials about their vacant coaching position, and received assurances from Penn State officials that he would be strongly considered as Engle's successor.

Paterno was appointed associate head coach before the 1964 season. He was hired as head coach one day after Engle announced his retirement in February 1966. He inherited a 5–5 team and went 5–5 in his first season, including a 15–7 victory over Maryland in a dreadful game at Beaver Stadium—his first game as head coach.

All-America defensive tackle Mike Reid registered three safeties in that game, which still stands as the school record for most in a career. Paterno sought out Maryland coach Lou Saban when the game ended, but he couldn't find him. But Saban did call the next day.

"Joe, I want to apologize," Paterno said Saban told him. "I didn't come out to shake your hand, but I was so angry. Both our teams stunk; mine just stunk worse than yours did."

Paterno began to wonder about his coaching ability and about his team when the Nittany Lions opened the 1967 season with a 23–22 loss to Navy, dropping his record to under .500. It was then that he made a dramatic decision that would shape Penn State for years to come.

The next week at Miami, Paterno gradually inserted five sophomores into the game on defense, joining tackle Steve Smear, who was also a sophomore. Linebackers Dennis Onkotz, Jim Kates, and Pete Johnson and defensive backs Paul Johnson and Neal Smith—along with Smear—became members of one of the most dominant defenses in Penn State history and turned out to be the backbone of a thirty-one-game unbeaten streak that started in Miami early in the 1967 season and ended the second game of the 1970 season.

They held opponents to nine points or less in eighteen of those games; only five teams scored twenty or more points against them. They beat some of the top offenses in the country, including those of Kansas in the 1969 Orange Bowl and Missouri in the 1970 Orange Bowl.

"Joe instilled in us how to win," said Vic Surma, an offensive tackle from 1968 to 1970. "He's a special man, a special person. There's nobody better in taking high school players and making them men. His forte is making good football players."

Despite posting back-to-back 11–0 seasons in 1968 and 1969, Penn State finished no better than second in the polls. Near the end of the 1969 season, then-President Nixon attended the game between number one Texas and number two Arkansas to present the winning team with a plaque symbolic of the national championship.

After Texas won 15–14, Nixon went to the Longhorns' locker room and presented them with the plaque. Paterno, the coach of third-ranked and unbeaten Penn State, was infuriated that the president didn't at least wait until the bowl games were played.

Four years later, when he was asked to be the speaker at Penn State's commencement, Paterno took a dig at Nixon, who was then embroiled in the Watergate scandal. "I'd like to know how could the president know so little about Watergate in 1973," Paterno said, "and so much about college football in 1969?"

By 1973 Paterno had established himself as one of the top coaches in the country and had become a hot commodity. The

New England Patriots asked him to be their head coach and general manager and offered a contract that would have made him a millionaire. He told Patriots' owner Billy Sullivan one night that he was going to accept the job, but he woke up the next morning with a change of heart and said no. "My decision virtually eliminates pro football from my career," Paterno said at a press conference in January 1973. "I think this is a decision I made with the idea that I'll stay here for the rest of my life."

That year, he led Penn State to its third unbeaten season in his first eight seasons as head coach. Tailback John Cappelletti, a defensive back earlier in his career, rushed for at least 200 yards in three straight games in November and ran off with the school's first Heisman Trophy.

The Lions went on to beat LSU 16–9 in the Orange Bowl and became the first team in school history to win twelve games. They were one of only two teams in the country with perfect records, but they finished fifth in the polls.

"We have as much right to claim the top place as anyone else," Paterno said. "We're undefeated. . . . I have my own poll—the Paterno Poll. The vote was unanimous—Penn State is Number One!"

The Nittany Lions finally gained their first number one ranking late in the 1978 season, which set up a showdown for the national championship against number two Alabama and coach Paul "Bear" Bryant in the Sugar Bowl. The game was a taut duel between two legendary defenses and two great coaches.

The Crimson Tide won 14–7 after stopping Matt Suhey and Mike Guman from inside the 1 on consecutive downs in the fourth quarter. The Lions had another chance to tie or win, but they had twelve men on the field when a shanked Alabama punt went out of bounds at the Tide 20.

Paterno remained in a funk over the loss for several months, pondered retirement, and wandered the streets of Brooklyn, where he grew up. He pitied himself for being outcoached by Bryant, and he was distant from the players the next season.

That year, 1979, Paterno sustained what might have been his most miserable season. He dealt with several injuries, several disciplinary problems, and his continuing hangover from the Alabama game. "It was a frustrating game," he said years later. "I didn't do a very good job of coaching. It still bugs me."

Paterno began the 1980s as an athletic director and ended it as an author. In between he led Penn State to a decade of unprecedented success and change. The Lions won their two national championships (in 1982 and 1986), suffered their first losing season (1988) in fifty years, and joined the Big Ten Conference after more than a century as an independent.

By the middle of the 1981 season, Penn State had regained the number one ranking and promptly lost it after two weeks with a 17–14 loss at Miami. With a strong-armed quarterback named Todd Blackledge, a swift tailback named Curt Warner, a powerful offensive line, and a bend-but-don't-break defense, the Lions had the makings of a very good team.

In 1982 they went 10–1 in the regular season against one of the nation's toughest schedules, losing only to Alabama and Bryant, Paterno's nemesis, and were ranked second. Another number one versus number two matchup was set for the Sugar Bowl, only this one against Georgia and Herschel Walker.

Penn State built a big lead in the first half and held on for a thrilling 27–23 victory. After three unbeaten and uncrowned seasons, the quest by Paterno and the Lions for their national title was finally over. "I don't think there is anything to be

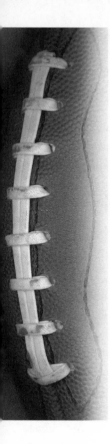

Bryant's Request

Penn State had faced Alabama twice in the Sugar Bowl in the 1970s before the Nittany Lions and the Crimson Tide began a 10-year series in 1981.

Legendary Alabama coach Paul "Bear" Bryant was preparing for his first trip to State College when he called Penn State coach Joe Paterno a few days before the game. Visiting teams flew into Harrisburg International Airport in those days and bused to State College.

"I hear it's a real tough bus ride from Harrisburg to State College," Bryant said on the phone.

"It's not fun, Coach," Paterno replied.

"You think you can call the governor and get one lane cleared out for us?" Bryant asked.

"I'll try," Paterno answered.

Bryant and the Crimson Tide made it to State College, even though one lane wasn't cleared out for them.

relieved of," Paterno said. "I felt satisfied all those years when we won them all. It wasn't my fault in those years that the votes weren't there."

Penn State played in two more number one versus number two bowl games for the national championship in 1985–86. The Lions posted an 11–0 regular season in 1985 behind a suffocating defense and a brainy quarterback named John Shaffer and vaulted to the top of the rankings again. But they lost to second-ranked Oklahoma 25–10 in the Orange Bowl.

Penn State entered the 1986 season with an experienced team, abundant confidence, and a ranking of sixth in the nation. The Lions were 6–0 and, according to their critics, untested when they traveled to play second-ranked Alabama. Although the Crimson Tide had the longest unbeaten streak in the country (thirteen games), Penn State pounded Alabama 23–3.

The Lions went on to beat Maryland, Notre Dame, and Pittsburgh and finished 11–0 in the regular season, setting up a showdown against fellow unbeaten Miami in the Fiesta Bowl. In a game billed as "The Duel in the Desert," underdog Penn State sacked Heisman Trophy winner Vinny Testaverde five times and intercepted him five times to beat the Hurricanes 14–10 and win its second national championship.

"I can't put into words how happy I am for these kids," he said then. "They worked hard, believed in themselves, and had the poise to withstand the pressure."

The 1986 season was Paterno's fourth perfect season and put him in a class with the great coaches in the history of the game. A few weeks before the Fiesta Bowl, *Sports Illustrated* named Paterno its Sportsman of the Year, making him the first college football coach to receive the honor. The American Football Coaches Association later named him Coach of the Year for a record fourth time.

The rest of the 1980s, though, was rocky for Penn State and Paterno, who endured his first losing season in 1988, several high-profile discipline issues, and injuries to key players.

"There were three ways I could go," he wrote in *Paterno: By the Book*, published before the 1989 season. "I could keep doing what we had always been doing and hope it would all get better. I could back out. Or I could start over."

Penn State was about to start over and reshape the landscape of college football. In December 1989 the school accepted an invitation to join the Big Ten Conference and end more than a century as an independent. The Lions began play in the Big Ten in 1993 and a new era that included another perfect season and a record-breaking victory.

After going 10–2 in its first season in the Big Ten, losing only to Michigan and Ohio State, Penn State entered the 1994 season as a contender in the conference, but not the favorite. But after scoring at least thirty-eight points in each of their first five games, the Lions moved to number three in the rankings and beat Michigan in their first trip to Michigan Stadium.

Two weeks later, they moved up to number one and trampled Ohio State, ranked number twenty-one, 63–14. Yet they fell to number two in one poll that week and were ranked second in the other poll after a six-point win at Indiana. Despite this, Penn State went on to win its first Big Ten championship and finish 11–0 in the regular season.

The Lions became Paterno's fourth undefeated and uncrowned team when they pounded Oregon 38–20 in the Rose Bowl and stayed second in the polls behind Nebraska, which beat Miami in the Orange Bowl. Paterno became the first coach to win the Rose, Orange, Sugar, and Cotton Bowls, but he was not completely satisfied.

"We proved to everyone in the country that we're certainly worthy to be national champions as much as anyone else," he said.

Penn State won at least nine games the next five seasons, but the Lions finished in the top ten only once, after a 38–15 romp past Texas in the Fiesta Bowl after the 1996 season. Paterno became the sixth major college to win 300 games

12   Stadium Stories

when Penn State routed Bowling Green in 1998, but his pursuit of another Big Ten title fell short.

In 1999, as he was drawing closer to Bryant's major college record of 323 coaching wins, Paterno led the Lions to victories in their first nine games and a number two ranking. But they lost consecutive games to Minnesota, Michigan, and Michigan State to fall out of contention for the national title, the Big Ten title, and the top ten.

Little did anyone know that those three games were the start of the worst stretch in Paterno's career. Penn State lost fourteen of twenty games from 1999 to 2001 and suffered back-to-back losing seasons.

The Lions started the 2001 season 0–4, the worst start in school history. They ranked last in the nation in scoring, total offense and rushing. And eleven months after their last win — in November 2000 — Paterno was still one win from tying Bryant.

During an off week Paterno finally gave the OK to implement the shotgun snap and the spread offense. The next week at Northwestern, Penn State came from behind five times to win 38–35 on freshman Zack Mills's short touchdown pass to Eric McCoo with twenty-two seconds left.

Paterno tied Bryant, then he passed him the next week. The Lions staged their biggest comeback at Beaver Stadium, rallying from eighteen points down to beat Ohio State 29–27. Mills passed for 280 yards and two touchdowns, ran for 138 yards and one touchdown, and broke the school record for total offense with 418 yards.

"I can't put into words what this football team, this town, this university mean to me," Paterno said. "I've had the greatest fifty-two years anyone has the right to expect. This football team could have packed it in a long time ago. But they didn't. I can't tell you how proud I am of them."

Joe Paterno addresses the Beaver Stadium crowd after Penn State's 29–27 win over Ohio State in 2001 gave him his record 324th victory. (Steve Manuel)

Penn State finished that season with five wins in its last seven games and went 9–4 in 2002, a year in which the Lions lost four games by a total of twenty points, including two in overtime. Now in his mid-seventies, Paterno had returned Penn State to its winning ways and maintained his enthusiasm for coaching.

"This game is like a gasoline for him," said Justin Kurpeikis, who played defensive end from 1997 to 2000. "It's a fuel for him. It's what keeps him so energetic and so intense."

Paterno is the all-time leader among coaches in bowl appearances (thirty-one) and bowl wins (twenty). Eighteen of his thirty-seven teams have won at least ten games; five of them have finished unbeaten. He received the Amos Alonzo Stagg Award from the American Football Coaches Association, its highest honor, and he became the first active coach to receive the Distinguished American Award from the National Football Foundation and College Football Hall of Fame.

His tenure at Penn State has spanned the administrations of eleven American presidents. Since Paterno became head coach in 1966, there have been more than 710 coaching changes at Division I schools, an average of more than six per school.

He has accomplished what he set out to do, establishing Penn State as a national power and as a program that has high academic standards. And when the 2002 season ended, he showed no signs of wanting to slow down.

"Joe wanted this to be a nationally successful program with intersectional success," said Jim Tarman, the former athletic director and sports information director. "He wanted this to be a different type of program. Well, he's been more than a football coach. Look at what he has done for the university.

"He wanted young people who belonged here and who worked toward graduation. Joe was so bright and so articulate and so good with people and with Xs and Os, I knew he was going to be the success he is."

Hall of Famers

M ike Munchak looked out from the stage at the Pro
Football Hall of Fame and saw the busloads of
people from his hometown of Scranton, Pennsylvania. He saw fans from Houston, where he spent his entire
NFL playing career.

Munchak looked to his right and to his left and saw child-
hood heroes and contemporaries. His football career flashed
before his eyes.

"I started at Penn State without knowing the offensive
guard position," Munchak said later. "I remembered how
many people helped me along the way to get there. That was
the biggest thing. I met Franco Harris, Jack Ham, and Lenny
Moore [at the induction ceremony]. That was a nice part, too.

"They acted like they've known me forever. I never met
those guys when I was at Penn State."

But Munchak will be grouped with Harris, Ham, and
Moore forever in an exclusive club. Those four and August
Michalske, who played professionally in the 1920s and 1930s,
represent Penn State in the Pro Football Hall of Fame.

"You feel like you never belong," said Munchak, who was
inducted in 2001. "It's like Fantasyland. 'Did that really
happen?' It was a phenomenal deal."

Mike Munchak

Mike Munchak played fullback and defensive end at Scranton
Central High School and weighed 225 pounds as a senior.

When he arrived at Penn State, he briefly played on the defensive line before the coaches moved him to the offensive line. He thought it was going to be a temporary move, but it turned out to be a little more than that.

By the time he was a sophomore, he weighed 265 pounds and started in 1979, missed the 1980 season with a knee injury, and returned as one of Penn State's foundations in 1981.

"I had never played offensive line in my life," Munchak recalled. "Once they moved me to the offensive line, Dick Anderson, my line coach, did a great job of preparing me. I was way ahead of a lot of people. I was going against Bruce Clark and Matt Millen in practice. It was a matter of survival."

Munchak teamed with Sean Farrell to give the Nittany Lions one of the best sets of guards in the country in 1981. Farrell had been named to an All-America team the previous season and was named to several All-America teams as a senior. He and Munchak paved the way for Curt Warner to rush for 1,000 yards.

In their last game together, Munchak and Farrell helped Penn State whip USC 26–10 in the Fiesta Bowl and finish third in the national rankings. Munchak had a year of eligibility left, but he decided to make himself available in the NFL draft.

The Houston Oilers drafted Munchak with the eighth overall pick, a few picks before the Tampa Bay Buccaneers took Farrell. "I wasn't really counting on Houston," Munchak said. "They caught me off guard. It was a thrill being drafted that high. The only guy I knew in Houston was Earl Campbell. I had never been to Texas."

Offensive guard Mike Munchak played twelve seasons in the NFL with the Houston Oilers and was named to the NFL's All-Decade Team for the 1980s.

Munchak immediately became a starter at left guard as the Oilers went 0–8–1 in his rookie year. But after acquiring such talent as Warren Moon, Alonzo Highsmith, Mike Rozier, Bruce Matthews, and Dean Steinkuhler over the next few years, the Oilers made the playoffs in 1987, starting a seven-year postseason run.

"Coming from Penn State, winning two or three games a year was kind of depressing," Munchak said. "When we finally made it and beat Seattle in a playoff game at the Astrodome, I realized the hard work paid off. [I said to myself] 'Now I know what this NFL is all about.'"

Munchak was selected to play in the Pro Bowl nine times and made the All-Pro team four times. He was named to the NFL All-Decade Team for the 1980s. He played from 1982 to 1993 and helped Houston win AFC Central championships in 1991 and 1993.

When he retired, Oilers general manager Floyd Reese asked him if he'd be interested in coaching. The Oilers wound up moving to Tennessee, and Munchak ended up on the Titans' staff as offensive line coach.

"I didn't want to coach," Munchak said. "I saw the hours they put in. I took over the quality control position at first. I enjoyed that. I felt real confident. I always thought I could coach in high school or college but not the NFL."

He helped the Titans reach the Super Bowl in 1999, but it didn't compare to his Hall of Fame induction. "When I was playing, it never crossed my mind [that I would go into the Hall of Fame]," Munchak said. "I was a lineman without many stats. I knew it would be hard. When I got the call, I wasn't even thinking it was possible. It was an unbelievable feeling."

Franco Harris

Franco Harris went to Penn State for an education, and he got one from Joe Paterno.

Paterno, the Nittany Lions coach, repeated sayings or slogans until they were ingrained in his players' heads. One of them led Harris to making one of the most famous plays in NFL history.

"Joe would always be mentioning, 'Go to the ball, that's where the action is,'" Harris recalled. "'That's where things happen. You might be able to recover the ball or throw a block.' I thought of that little voice from the first time I stepped on the Steelers' practice field. It became instinctive.

"Because of that, the 'Immaculate Reception' happened."

The 6'2", 230-pound Harris caught a pass that may or may not have bounced off a group of players downfield—depending on who's telling the story—and sprinted into the end zone to give the Pittsburgh Steelers a shocking 13–7 playoff win over the Oakland Raiders in 1972, his rookie season. He went on to enjoy an outstanding twelve-year career in the NFL and was inducted into the Pro Football Hall of Fame in 1990.

He helped the Steelers win four Super Bowl championships and was named the Player of the Decade for the 1970s by *College & Pro Football Newsweekly*. Like his Penn State and Steelers teammate Jack Ham, drafted a year ahead of him, Harris did not want to play pro ball in Pittsburgh.

"I grew up in New Jersey and played at Penn State," he said. "I wanted a change of scenery. I wanted to see other parts of the country. Pittsburgh was at the bottom of my list. They had more losing seasons than any other team in NFL history. I wasn't excited about coming here."

The Steelers took Harris with the thirteenth pick in the 1972 draft. At Penn State, Harris played fullback and was over-shadowed by halfback Lydell Mitchell, who ran for nearly 1,600 yards and scored twenty-nine touchdowns in their senior year in 1971.

Harris still finished his career with 2,002 rushing yards and twenty-four touchdowns while playing with Mitchell and also Charlie Pittman in 1969 in the same backfield. That season, Harris had a big game at Syracuse, running for a two-point conversion and then scoring the game-winning 36-yard touchdown for a 15–14 win. "That was pretty exciting for me," he said. "It was a big win. When everything seemed lost, when things didn't look good, it was time to perform."

Harris performed quite well in the NFL, going to nine straight Pro Bowls (1972–80), the only player in the league to be so honored. At one time, he held twenty-nine NFL records and remains the all-time leader in postseason rushing yards with 1,556 in nineteen games. He also was named the MVP of Super Bowl IX.

"We had incredible talent that played as a team," Harris said. "No one tried to be bigger than the team. Not only were they great athletes and great players, they also were great people. That made us very close. They were people who you liked to be around.

"I always enjoyed the first championship and the excite-ment of going there. It was just a wonderful experience. We enjoyed it so much, we said, 'Let's do this again and again and again.' "

Running back Franco Harris helped lead the Pittsburgh Steelers to four Super Bowl championships and was chosen the Player of the Decade for the 1970s by one publication.

Harris played with the Steelers from 1972 to 1983 and finished his career with the Seattle Seahawks in 1984. He had eight 1,000-yard seasons, 12,120 career yards, and 100 career touchdowns.

"I really achieved what I wanted to achieve," he said. "That makes me feel good. I guess I would say that I was a guy who lived his dream in everything that the game had to offer."

It all started in December 1972 when he caught a deflected pass and scored the most significant touchdown in the history of the Steelers.

"Barry Pearson was the primary receiver and Bradshaw ended up throwing the ball to Frenchy Fuqua," he recalled. "There was a big collision. I heard that little voice in my head say, 'Go to the ball.'

"Things just seemed to jell. We [had] the best season ever for the Steelers (11–3) till that point. It was a phenomenal year. It was a magical year."

Jack Ham

Jack Ham grew up in Johnstown, less than two hours from Pittsburgh, and played college football at Penn State, less than three hours from Pittsburgh. But he was disappointed when the Steelers picked him in the second round of the 1971 draft.

"I wasn't much of a Pittsburgh fan," Ham said. "I lived near there my entire life. I thought maybe playing somewhere else would give me the opportunity to live at least six months in another area of the country. And I was a little bit disappointed that I was drafted in the second round."

Ham's disappointment faded away when he helped the Steelers, once laughingstocks of the NFL, win four Super Bowl championships in the 1970s. He became the only linebacker to be selected to the Pro Bowl for eight straight seasons in that decade and was inducted into the Pro Football Hall of Fame in 1988.

He enjoyed an outstanding career with the Steelers and with Penn State, where he was offered the last scholarship available to the class of 1967. With the Nittany Lions he became a starter as a sophomore in 1968 and played on back-to-back undefeated teams in 1968 and 1969. He was named a first-team All-American in 1970.

"I never realized how important the mental part of the game is until I got to Penn State," Ham said. "With Dan Radakovich, Jerry Sandusky, and Joe [Paterno] sticklers for details, they made sure I knew that athletic ability kind of levels off in major college football. It's who does and doesn't make mental errors in the third and fourth quarters who ends up winning games."

Ham, who blocked four punts in his career, made ninety-one tackles and four interceptions as a senior. He later was inducted into the College Football Hall of Fame. At Penn State he built a reputation as a thinking man's linebacker, making plays with his brains and his talent. "You learn, so you're anticipating a play instead of guessing it," he said. "I kind of prided myself on preparation, looking at tape and having some quickness as well. I made sure I was not surprised by anything out there."

Ham, 6'2", 225 as a pro, immediately became a starter with the Steelers, who had suffered through decades of losing. Pittsburgh fans came out sporadically until the Steelers began to win. Ham's rookie year in 1971 was the last time in his twelve-year career they did not sell out Three Rivers Stadium.

"The town kind of identified with us, especially our defense," Ham said of the "Steel Curtain." "Today they think that Ham never missed a tackle and that [Terry] Bradshaw

Linebacker Jack Ham was selected to play in the Pro Bowl eight straight times and was a unanimous choice on the All-Decade Team for the 1970s.

never threw an interception. The Pirates were winning, too, so people took a lot of pride being from Pittsburgh.

"Everybody on our team had a fan club, even the backup players."

Ham made two interceptions in the 1974 AFC Championship Game and was named the NFL Defensive Player of the Year in 1975. He had twenty-five and a half sacks, twenty-one fumble recoveries, and thirty-two interceptions in his career, which ended in 1982. He was a unanimous selection to the All-NFL Team of the Decade for the 1970s.

"I have a whole bunch of teammates in the Hall of Fame," Ham said. "I'm considered a great linebacker because Joe Greene and L. C. Greenwood played in front of me.

"I'm most proud of winning back-to-back Super Bowls twice. Sometimes you can sneak up on people. It's special to be able to come back and do it again when everybody is gunning for you."

Lenny Moore

For Lenny Moore it was just another game on the schedule in his senior year at Penn State. For the 30,321 people who watched the November 5, 1955, game at Beaver Field, it was one of the most memorable games they had ever seen.

Moore carried twenty-two times for 146 yards and one touchdown to lead the Nittany Lions past rival Syracuse 21–20. Jim Brown, who like Moore would go on to a great NFL career, rushed twenty times for 159 yards and scored all of the Orangemen's points, but Penn State won.

"It was a big game for us probably because Jim Brown was really coming into his own," Moore said. "We beat them and

Moore Passes Test

I t didn't take long for Lenny Moore to make an impression on his Penn State coaches and teammates. After arriving in Happy Valley in 1952, Moore immediately showed the skills and savvy that eventually landed him in the Pro Football Hall of Fame. While a freshman on the scout team, he gave the first team defense fits with his speed and moves.

"Nobody knew how tough he was," said Joe Paterno, then a Penn State assistant coach. "Nobody could tackle him. He'd get in the secondary and give a little bit of this (shoulder fake) and everybody would be on their faces."

One day, though, Moore was trapped between defensive end Rosey Grier, who was two years ahead of Moore, and a cornerback.

"I'm standing behind the offense calling plays," Paterno said. "Here comes Lenny around the outside. Grier comes off the block and Grier's got him. Lenny has no place to go. Either he runs out of bounds or he lets Rosey get a shot at him.

"Lenny's not gonna run out of bounds. Lenny turns up and I can still see Rosey's face light up. He goes, 'You son of a gun. I got ya. I got ya.' Rosey was a big man for then, a 250-pounder, and he knocks over Lenny, kills him.

"Lenny gets right up and says, 'Not bad for an old man.' We knew we had a great football player."

they even tried to start a little fight after the game. I never thought about me. I never thought that I did this or that."

His humility aside, Moore was one of the greatest running backs and defensive backs in Penn State history. He went on to enjoy a marvelous pro career with the Baltimore Colts and was inducted into the Pro Football Hall of Fame in 1975.

He still ranks in the top ten in NFL history with 113 touchdowns and gained 12,451 yards as a rusher and receiver. He was named to the All-NFL team five times and played in seven Pro Bowls.

"I was drafted as a defensive back [with the ninth pick overall in 1956]," Moore recalled. "So when I went down to Baltimore, they gave me a little look-see. Weeb [Ewbank, the Colts' coach] had guys throw me a couple pitchouts. And then he threw me a couple flare passes.

"We only had thirty-three players on the roster. Weeb had all his backs learn how to run pass routes with wide receivers in case we were short. I was on the kickoff team, the kickoff return team, and the punt return team. I was the safety man in our prevent defense."

Moore ran for 7.5 yards a carry and eight touchdowns and caught eleven passes in 1956 and was named the Rookie of the Year. Two years later, he helped the Colts win the NFL championship with an overtime victory over the New York Giants. He suffered a chest injury early in the game but remained on the field. "I was a decoy most of the game," he said. "I couldn't make a lot of turns and movements. Weeb said, 'Don't say anything.' My job was to occupy the cornerback and safety on my side of the field. I took them out of the picture. That put Raymond Berry in more one-on-one situations."

A year later, the Colts easily beat New York in Baltimore for their second straight championship. Moore continued to be one of the most versatile and dangerous offensive players in the league until he suffered a head injury midway through the 1963 season.

He came back the next season with a vengeance, running for 584 yards and sixteen touchdowns, while catching twenty-one passes for 472 yards and three touchdowns. He was named the Comeback Player of the Year and was voted the league MVP by the players. "I cherished the MVP award," Moore said. "It was probably the highest award I received as a player. I know the sacrifices I had to make to make it a reality."

He scored touchdowns in a record eighteen straight games from 1963 to 1965 and retired after the 1967 season. "I knew things were coming to an end," he said. "I started thinking on the field. When I looked at the film, the truth was there. I thought I was doing things like I always did them. But when I watched film, my legs reacted slowly."

Eight years later, Lenny "Spats" Moore, nicknamed for the white tape he used on his low-cut shoes, was voted into the Hall of Fame. "That alone gives credence to people," he said. "They will remember you as one of the best ever and I had nothing to do with that."

August "Mike" Michalske

The first Penn State player inducted into the Hall of Fame, in 1964, Michalske played guard and fullback at Penn State from 1923 to 1925.

He was first an outstanding offensive guard and defensive lineman. He was moved to fullback in the middle of his senior year because of his size (6', 206 pounds) and speed. He scored both touchdowns in Penn State's 13–6 win over Michigan State in 1925.

He played professionally with the New York (football) Yankees from 1926 to 1928 before moving onto the Green Bay Packers (1929–35, 1937), where he helped the Packers win three NFL championships. He was named to the All-NFL team six times. He coached college football for several years before coaching with the Baltimore Colts. He died in 1983.

Tailback Blue

T he tailback tradition at Penn State that stretches back
fifty years may have started with the arrival of Lenny
Moore in 1952.

Moore enjoyed an outstanding career with the Nittany
Lions, playing in the offensive and defensive backfield from
1953 to 1955. He had breakaway speed and pillowy hands,
becoming the first Penn State back to rush for 1,000 yards in a
season and the school's all-time leading rusher.

After the Colts picked him in the first round in 1956, he
helped Baltimore win two NFL championships and scored
113 touchdowns. While Moore earned his way into the Pro
Football Hall of Fame, two kids in the Baltimore area followed
his career with great interest—Charlie Pittman and Lydell
Mitchell, who went on to star at Penn State.

"I was a die-hard Baltimore Colts fan," Pittman said, "and
Lenny Moore was one of my heroes. He had a big influence
on why I decided to go to Penn State."

"The Baltimore Colts were a great team back then,"
Mitchell said. "I knew a lot about him. I met him for the first
time when I was a sophomore at Penn State. He came down to
a game at the Naval Academy. We took pictures with him. I'll
never forget that."

Moore planted the seed for Penn State's storied tailback
tradition, and Pittman, Mitchell, and Franco Harris gave it
roots when they played in the same backfield in 1969. Then it
was John Cappelletti, Curt Warner, D. J. Dozier, Blair
Thomas, Ki-Jana Carter, Curtis Enis, and Larry Johnson, each

Lenny Moore began Penn State's tailback tradition and rushed for 2,380 yards from 1953 to 1955.

one of them a first-team All-American, and each one of them playing a role in the Lions' success under coach Joe Paterno.

"When Penn State's running game is clicking, they're almost unbeatable," Pittman said. "That's been the hallmark of Joe's success. When we can run the football well and can have a dominant tailback, we can be successful. When we don't have a dominant tailback, we haven't been successful."

Penn State's tailbacks usually have been overshadowed by its linebackers, which include eleven All-Americans in the Paterno era. While Penn State is often called "Linebacker U.," the moniker "Tailback U." has often been reserved for Southern California.

"When you think about Penn State, you always think about the linebackers," Mitchell said. "But we had a lot of good running backs go through there. I think people got so much into the linebackers, they had a tendency to forget about the tailbacks who have come through there."

The 6', 185-pound Moore was Penn State's first great back of the second half of the twentieth century. A native of Reading, Pennsylvania, he led the Lions in rushing in each of his three seasons and posted his best year in 1954 when he gained 1,082 yards, averaged 8 yards per carry, and ranked second in the nation in rushing.

He also made ten career interceptions on defense, leading Penn State as a junior and a senior when two-way football was the rule. In a 13–0 win over Pittsburgh in 1954, he had two interceptions and a fumble recovery.

In one of the great duels of that era, he rushed for 146 yards and one touchdown in a 21–20 win over Jim Brown and Syracuse. Brown ran for 159 yards, scored all three Orangemen touchdowns, and kicked two extra points.

With his high-stepping style, Moore finished his career with 2,380 rushing yards and twenty-three touchdowns and ranks eleventh on Penn State's all-time rushing list. Yet he was never selected as a first-team All-American.

"Lenny was phenomenal," Pittman said. "He could flat-out fly. He wasn't big. He wasn't overpowering. But he was elusive."

Eleven years after Moore's career at Penn State ended, Pittman arrived in Happy Valley and asked to wear number 24, the number Moore wore with the Colts. The Lions had some good backs in the years between Moore and Pittman, but none made a huge impact.

The 6'1", 190-pound Pittman, an outstanding student, chose to attend Penn State over Maryland, Navy, and several Ivy League schools at a time when the school's minority enrollment was low. A few years ago, Pittman commissioned an artist to do a drawing of Penn State's great running backs and asked Paterno to sign it.

"He joked with me and said, 'Charlie, you couldn't even make my team today,'" Pittman recalled. "I said, 'If I hadn't come here, they wouldn't have been here.' Joe said I was right. I sort of paved the way for others to come to Penn State and be successful."

Pittman played wingback as a sophomore in 1967 and gained a team-high 580 yards. He moved to halfback in 1968 and enjoyed his finest season, rushing for 950 yards and fourteen touchdowns. He then played in the same backfield with Mitchell and Harris as a senior and led the Lions for the third straight year with 706 yards.

"I don't care who we played, they could not focus on any one back," Pittman said. "Any of the three could kill you. Joe figured out how to get us enough touches. He managed that quite well."

The day he, Mitchell, and Harris met Moore at Navy, Pittman enjoyed his greatest game with 177 yards and two touchdowns. He helped Penn State post back-to-back 11–0 seasons and was named a first-team All-American in 1969.

"We didn't know what it was like to lose," Pittman said. "I think we had great friendships. We enjoyed each other. We hung out with each other. We respected one another's ability."

Pittman ranks twelfth on the Lions' career rushing list with 2,239 yards and went on to play two seasons in the NFL before injuries forced him to retire.

When Mitchell and Harris visited Penn State on a recruiting trip, Pittman was one of their hosts. Mitchell also was considering Ohio State and couldn't make up his mind.

"Joe told him that the only reason he wouldn't go to Penn State was because he couldn't beat out Charlie Pittman," Pittman recalled. "Joe used that carrot to attract Lydell."

The 6', 198-pound Mitchell used his quick feet and shifty moves to pass Moore and become Penn State's all-time leading rusher for a time with 2,934 yards.

He had a tremendous senior year in 1971 when he rushed for 1,567 yards, a school record until Larry Johnson broke it in 2002, and twenty-six touchdowns. He rushed for at least 100 yards in eight of Penn State's eleven games and scored at least one touchdown in all but one game. He led the nation in scoring with twenty-nine touchdowns and 174 points, which remain school records.

A three-year starter, Mitchell was named an All-American as a senior and finished fifth in the Heisman Trophy voting.

"My style probably resembled Ki-Jana out of all the other Penn State backs," Mitchell said. "I made quick moves and tried to make people miss. Very seldom did the first man bring me down. I was supposed to make him miss."

"It was a wonderful opportunity to play in a backfield with Lydell and Charlie," Franco Harris has said of his Penn State days. "I used to watch Charlie a lot and got a lot from him. Maybe he didn't know it, but I was a student of his. It helped me later on."

The 6'2", 220-pound Franco Harris, who grew up in Mount Holly, New Jersey, enjoyed a good career at Penn State

One Vote for Mitchell

Charlie Pittman has followed Penn State football since graduating from there in 1970 and ranks among the Nittany Lions' greatest running backs.

Penn State has had nine All-America backs since Joe Paterno became head coach in 1966, including Pittman. If he had to pick the best he has seen, Pittman says he would choose Lydell Mitchell.

"He was an incredible runner," Pittman said of his backup in 1969. "He was so tough. I remember telling him to avoid contact. 'You gotta glance off people and don't take so many direct hits.' He kept getting up."

Mitchell ranks sixth in Penn State history with 2,934 yards from 1969–71. He played behind Pittman one year and with Franco Harris for three years. John Cappelletti, who won Penn State's only Heisman Trophy in 1973, was forced to play defensive back until Mitchell graduated.

"I think Lenny Moore (1953–55) and Curt Warner (1979–82) were great," Pittman said, "but Lydell made the Heisman Trophy winner (Cappelletti) play defense."

before he went on to become one of the great backs in NFL history. With the Lions he played fullback and rushed for 2,002 yards and twenty-four touchdowns while playing in the shadow of Mitchell and Pittman.

He posted his finest game in 1971 at Iowa when he gained 145 yards and scored four touchdowns. On three occasions he and Mitchell each rushed for at least 100 yards in the same game.

The presence of Mitchell kept a promising running back named John Cappelletti in the defensive backfield for his first two seasons. Cappelletti, a native of Upper Darby, Pennsylvania, even started on defense as a sophomore before Mitchell left and he moved to offense in 1972.

That year, Cappelletti ran for 1,117 yards and twelve touchdowns with his bruising, punishing style. At 6'1", 225 pounds, he was deceptively fast and very strong. After helping Penn State reach the Sugar Bowl, he became ill in New Orleans and missed the game, his absence a factor in the Lions' 14–0 loss to Oklahoma.

The next year, 1973, Cappelletti got off to a good start with four 100-yard outings in Penn State's first seven games. No one, though, predicted what he was about to do in the final four games in November. He ran for 202 yards against Maryland, 220 against North Carolina State, 204 against Ohio University, and 161 against Pitt, making a huge late-season push.

He finished the year with 1,522 yards and seventeen touchdowns and became the Lions' first Heisman Trophy winner. He made it an even more memorable year when in his Heisman acceptance speech he paid tribute to his younger brother, Joey, who was stricken with leukemia.

Cappelletti ranks ninth on Penn State's career rushing list with 2,639 yards and twenty-nine touchdowns, despite playing on offense just two seasons. He's one of only four Penn State backs with consecutive 1,000-yard seasons, joining Warner, Carter, and Enis.

"You're talking about guys in the early years, like Lenny Moore, Charlie Pittman, Lydell Mitchell, and Franco Harris, who were talented athletes," Cappelletti said. "Those guys laid the foundation. Couple that with the style of offense that Joe runs, now you have a situation very conducive to successful running backs."

Matt Suhey, who played tailback and fullback from 1976 to 1979 at Penn State, was a steady, productive back who finished his career with 2,818 yards and twenty-six touchdowns. He rushed for 973 yards as a senior in 1979, the same year a tailback from a small town in West Virginia made his debut.

The 6', 208-pound Curt Warner was highly recruited and quickly showed why when he ran for 100 yards and two touchdowns, caught two passes for 71 yards and one touchdown, and gained 109 return yards in a 45–10 win over Rutgers in the 1979 opener.

Warner, a four-year starter, might have been the best all-around back in Penn State history. He posted consecutive 1,000-yard seasons in 1981 and 1982 and was twice named a first-team All-American.

In 1981 Warner ran for 238 yards in a victory over Nebraska and three weeks later ran for 256 yards in a win over Syracuse, a school record that stood until Johnson broke it in 2002.

He outdueled Heisman Trophy winners in back-to-back bowl games. In the 1982 Fiesta Bowl, he gained 145 yards against Southern Cal, compared with 85 yards for the Trojans' Marcus Allen. In the 1983 Sugar Bowl, he gained 117 yards against Georgia, compared with 103 for the Bulldogs' Herschel Walker.

Curt Warner, Penn State's all-time leading rusher with 3,398 yards from 1979 to 1982, outdueled Heisman Trophy winners Marcus Allen and Herschel Walker in bowl games.

Warner, who enjoyed an outstanding pro career with Seattle and Los Angeles, remains Penn State's all-time leading rusher with 3,398 yards.

D. J. Dozier, who had an upright running style, took over the tailback position in 1983 and promptly rushed for 1,002 yards, the only true freshman to top 1,000 yards at Penn State.

He posted four consecutive 100-yard games in the middle of that season against Iowa, Rutgers, Temple, and Alabama, gaining a career-high 196 against the Crimson Tide.

He slipped to 691 yards as a sophomore before rebounding with strong seasons in 1985 and 1986 when the Lions played for the national championship. Against Miami in the Fiesta Bowl, Dozier ran for 99 yards and caught two passes for 21 yards in Penn State's dramatic 14–10 win. It was his 6-yard touchdown run in the fourth quarter that provided the difference.

"The thing that sticks in my mind is the run he had against Miami," former Penn State defensive coordinator Jerry Sandusky said. "He stuttered and made a great run."

The 6'1", 210-pound Dozier remains the only player to lead the Lions in rushing four straight seasons. He ranks fourth in Penn State history with 3,227 career yards.

"It's an honor to be part of the tradition," Dozier said. "I knew Booker Moore, Lydell Mitchell, and Franco Harris from the pros. I knew when I went to Penn State that it would be a great challenge. We don't argue with people from other schools about who's Tailback U. Penn State obviously has had the best tailbacks."

Before Dozier went on to the NFL, where he played five seasons with Minnesota and Detroit, he offered advice to Blair Thomas, who was a sophomore on the 1986 team.

"I told Blair that it was a call to duty," said Dozier. "When he first went there, you noticed right away that he was talented, strong, and smart. He obviously did a great job."

Blair Thomas, a 5'11", 190-pound native of Philadelphia, saw limited playing time as a freshman before he averaged a school-record 8.4 yards per carry in the 1986 championship season. That year, he made a 92-yard run against Syracuse, which remains a school record.

Blair Thomas rushed for 3,301 yards in his career from 1985 to 1989 and gained 186 yards against BYU in the 1989 Holiday Bowl, a Penn State bowl record.

After Dozier left, Thomas rushed for 1,414 yards and eleven touchdowns in 1987 before suffering a knee injury in preparation for the Citrus Bowl. He sat out the 1988 season to recover and came back the following season to gain 1,341 yards and a place on an All-America team.

That year, he carried thirty-five times for 160 yards against Alabama, running the ball ten times in a row to within inches of the Crimson Tide goal line in the final minutes. Alabama, though, blocked a field goal try to preserve a 17–16 victory. Later, Thomas gained 186 yards in a wild 50–39 win over Brigham Young in the Holiday Bowl, the most by any Penn State back in a bowl game.

"I really didn't start understanding the rich tradition [at Penn State] until my junior year of high school," Thomas said. "I really started taking an interest in the program then. I wanted to be one of the great backs there."

Thomas played six seasons in the NFL with the New York Jets, who took him with the second pick of the 1990 draft, New England, Dallas, and Carolina, but his career was cut short by injuries. Now an assistant football coach at Temple, he ranks second on Penn State's career rushing list with 3,301 yards and twenty-one touchdowns.

Two years after Thomas left, three outstanding high school running backs enrolled at Penn State: Ki-Jana Carter, Mike Archie, and Stephen Pitts. They battled one another and shared playing time until Carter emerged as the best of the group in 1993.

The 5'11", 212-pound Carter, who grew up in suburban Columbus, Ohio, chose Penn State over Ohio State. With his blazing speed and his excellent vision, he was one of the most exciting backs the Lions have had. In 1993 he had seven 100-yard games and gained 1,026 yards, averaging 6.6 yards per carry.

The next year, Carter ran for at least 100 yards in ten out of twelve games, starting with 210 yards in the opener at Minnesota. He finished with 1,539 yards and twenty-three touchdowns, ranking second in the nation in scoring with 138 points and fourth in rushing. He averaged nearly 8 yards a carry.

He capped the regular season by running for 227 yards and five touchdowns against Michigan State. In the Rose Bowl he helped Penn State cap its perfect season when he burst 83 yards for a touchdown on the Lions' first play from scrimmage in a 38–20 win over Oregon. He shared the game MVP award after he gained 156 yards and scored three touchdowns.

He ranks seventh all-time at Penn State with 2,829 yards and likely would have broken Warner's record if he had stayed for his senior year. He finished second in voting for the Heisman Trophy and was the number one pick of the 1995 NFL draft, but a series of injuries have hampered him.

"He was a great team player," Paterno said of Carter. "He was always there when we needed him. He never gave me any lip. He was never bigger than the program. He was a delight to coach."

Curtis Enis began his Penn State career as a linebacker the next year. That experiment lasted one game before the 6'1", 231-pounder from Union City, Ohio, was moved to tailback for good. Like Franco Harris a quarter century before him, Enis was a hybrid. He had enough speed to run past defenders and enough strength to knock them over.

He averaged 6 yards a carry as a freshman while alternating with Archie and Pitts before he took over the job in 1996. In the Kickoff Classic that year, Enis opened some eyes when he erupted for a career-high 241 yards and three touchdowns against USC. He finished the year with 1,210 yards and thirteen TDs.

Enis started slowly in 1997 before running for at least 100 yards in each one of Penn State's eight Big Ten games and was named the conference's Offensive Player of the Year. His finest moment came when he carried twenty-three times for 211 yards in a thrilling 31–27 victory over Ohio State. He wound up with 1,363 yards and scored nineteen TDs.

Enis, also an outstanding receiver out of the backfield, was a finalist for the Doak Walker Award and was named to several All-America teams. But a few weeks before Penn State played Florida in the Citrus Bowl, he accepted gifts from an agent and was kept out of the game, ending his career in shame.

Enis finished his career with 3,256 yards, the third-best total in Penn State history. The Chicago Bears drafted him in the first round, but he retired after suffering several injuries during a brief career.

The next year, Larry Johnson was one of three running backs to enroll at Penn State and was the only to be redshirted that year. The 6'2", 222-pound Johnson, son of Lions' assistant coach Larry Johnson Sr., waited his turn, sometimes not patiently.

"At times I was frustrated," Johnson said. "I learned to be patient and to stay within the program."

When his turn came in 2002, Johnson made up for lost time. He became the ninth back in Division I-A history and the first in the Big Ten to rush for 2,000 yards in a regular season, gaining 2,015. He was outstanding in the first half of the season and incredible in the second half.

Johnson gained 257 yards against Northwestern, bettering Warner's single-game record by 1 yard. He surpassed the old record three more times, running for 279 against Illinois, 327 against Indiana, and 279 against Michigan State. On his final carry of the regular season, late in the second quarter of the win over the Spartans, he sprinted 38 yards for a touchdown to top 2,000 yards.

He averaged 8 yards per carry, led the nation in rushing and scoring, was a consensus All-American, won the Maxwell Award and the Doak Walker Award, and finished third in voting for the Heisman. He also caught thirty-nine passes for 341 yards and three touchdowns, a school record for receptions by a running back.

"To go through what he went through, to come in at the midnight hour, to accomplish what he has accomplished is tremendous," said Dozier, who befriended Johnson during his career. "We talked about where he would stand upon all that tradition. The question now is how far he will stand above those behind him."

Johnson finished his career with 2,953 yards, fifth on the Lions' all-time list. He ranks among the greatest backs in Penn State history and added to the legacy. If asked, he said he will offer advice to those who follow him.

"You have to be yourself," Johnson said. "You have to go out there and play hard. It's not just a game. Playing running back is a demanding job."

Linebacker U.

As an outstanding high school linebacker in western
Pennsylvania, Brandon Short wanted to attend Penn
State because he thought it was the best fit for him. He
had heard of the nickname Linebacker U., but he didn't fully
understand what it meant until after he got to Happy Valley.

"It's a deep and storied tradition, more than I first
thought," Short said. "Coach Sandusky had great pride in the
name 'Linebacker U.' Linebackers had to be held to a higher
standard in his mind."

Jerry Sandusky, the longtime defensive coordinator at
Penn State, returned to his alma mater to coach linebackers
in 1970, one year after Dennis Onkotz was named an All-
American for the second straight year.

Onkotz and former linebackers coach Dan Radakovich,
who left the Penn State staff after the 1969 season, began the
tradition. Sandusky enhanced it, going on to coach ten All-
America linebackers over the next thirty years, starting with
Jack Ham in 1970 and ending with Short in 1999.

"It started before me," said Ham, who went on to enjoy a
Hall of Fame career as a pro with the Pittsburgh Steelers.
"Denny Onkotz and Jim Kates were ahead of me. You want to
make sure you uphold the tradition. If you clump all the guys
who have played there, there are a lot of quality linebackers.

"It mushroomed after I left. I do take pride in that."

The Nittany Lions had seven All-America linebackers
from 1968 to 1976: Onkotz, Ham, Charlie Zapiec, John
Skorupan, Ed O'Neil, Greg Buttle, and Kurt Allerman. Shane

Conlan (1985–86), Andre Collins (1989), LaVar Arrington (1998–99), and Short received All-America honors later.

"Jack took me under his wing," Skorupan said of Ham. "We were fraternity brothers. He and Gary Hull, we'd go to their apartment and look at films. They showed me what to expect. When I was a senior, I took Buttle under my wing and did the same thing."

But it all started with Radakovich, who coached Sandusky when he was a player in the early 1960s. According to Onkotz, Radakovich instilled freedom, confidence and intelligence in his linebackers. The defense in those years overwhelmed opponents and carried Penn State to perfect seasons in 1968 and 1969.

"Dan was great at analyzing the opposition," Onkotz recalled. "I knew what the other teams were going to do, just by the personnel they had on the field. He had a very great mind for the game. Any halftime adjustments were great.

"We were well disciplined and well coached. The little things that he taught us allowed us to be a little bit better than the other guy."

After Onkotz graduated and Radakovich left, Sandusky returned to Penn State and had a veteran linebacking corps that included Ham, Hull, and Gary Gray. Sandusky learned as much from them as they learned from him.

"My sophomore year was Jerry's first year as a linebacker coach," Skorupan said. "It was a trip. Jack was a senior. Jerry would say, 'Let's go out and do this drill.' Jack said, 'No, we don't want to do that.' Jerry wasn't much older than us."

But Sandusky settled into the job and eventually became regarded as one of the top assistant coaches in the country. He often would take high school tight ends and defensive backs and turn them into linebackers. For example, Skorupan,

O'Neil, Conlan, and Collins played other positions before they moved to linebacker at Penn State. Sandusky always seemed to be looking for speed and intelligence from his players.

"You had to be an outstanding athlete to play linebacker at Penn State," Sandusky said. "They had to be fundamentally sound. I put together what I consider some fundamental principles of play. Those were things that could not be violated. We wanted them to be reckless and not robotic."

All eleven All-America linebackers went on to play in the NFL, some longer than others. Ham became the most celebrated, helping the Pittsburgh Steelers win four Super Bowl championships and becoming a unanimous selection on the NFL Team of the Decade for the 1970s.

At least twenty-one other Penn State linebackers went on to play in the NFL from 1969 to 2002.

"It was such an easy transition for me going from college to the NFL because I had it all," Skorupan said. "We had the techniques, the reads. Everything was instilled in us. I saw so many guys who came to the pros who were lost. We were taught the stance, the reads, and how to get rid of the blocks.

"Playing at Penn State gave me an advantage on some of the other guys who play my position. Our defense was so complicated at Penn State. We were asked to do a lot. We had to play the run, play receivers, cover backs out of the backfield. We did a lot more than other schools did. It prepared us better for the NFL."

Of course, despite the Nittany Lions' strong tradition, players from other schools suggest that Penn State isn't Linebacker U. "I get it from the Miami and the Michigan guys," Short said. "I tell them, 'We're Linebacker U. for a reason.'"

While Sandusky enjoyed tremendous success over the years, including Penn State's 14–10 win over high-powered Miami in the 1987 Fiesta Bowl, he's most proud of the people who have played the linebacker position at Penn State.

"So many of them became successful people," he said, "whether going into professional football or life. We had a lot of bright people who were outgoing and aggressive. They would be successful in any endeavor."

Here's a profile on each of Penn State's All-America linebackers:

Dennis Onkotz (1968-69)

A native of Northampton, Pennsylvania, Onkotz played a huge role in Penn State's back-to-back unbeaten seasons in 1968 and 1969.

Not a terribly big linebacker, Onkotz might have enjoyed his finest season as a sophomore in 1967 when he made 118 tackles and intercepted six passes, including two that he returned for touchdowns. In 1968 he had seventy-two tackles and four interceptions, including one that he ran back for a score. As a senior in 1969, he had ninety-seven tackles and one interception.

Onkotz ranks third in career tackles at Penn State with 287, trailing only Greg Buttle and Brian Gelzheiser. He's tied for eighth in career interceptions with eleven and shares the record for most interceptions returned for touchdown, three, with Darren Perry.

Dennis Onkotz, a two-time All-America linebacker in 1968 and 1969, returned three interceptions and two punts for touchdowns in his career.

He also returned punts in his career, running back two for touchdowns. He has the eighth-best career punt return average (13.2) at Penn State. Injuries cut short his professional career after the New York Jets drafted him in 1970.

Jack Ham (1970)

Ham, a native of Johnstown, Pennsylvania, is the only former Penn State player who is a member of the College Football Hall of Fame and Pro Football Hall of Fame.

After receiving the last scholarship available in 1967, Ham became a starter as a sophomore and helped the Nittany Lions post back-to-back 11–0 records in 1968 and 1969. He had ninety-five tackles as a junior when Penn State held opponents to ninety points and ninety-one tackles and four interceptions as a senior in 1970 when he was a unanimous All-America selection.

With Andre Collins, he shares the school record for blocked punts in a season, three in 1968, and in a career, four from 1968 to 1970. He ranks eleventh in Penn State history with 251 career tackles.

He went on to enjoy a Hall of Fame career with Pittsburgh, helping the Steelers win four NFL championships. He was named to the Pro Bowl nine years in a row and was named the NFL's Defensive Player of the Year in 1975.

"He had just fantastic instincts," Sandusky said. "He had spring and explosiveness. He was able to jump and make interceptions. He had tremendous football sense and savvy."

Charlie Zapiec (1971)

A Philadelphia native, Zapiec probably was the most unlikely of Penn State's All-America linebackers. He spent his first two seasons (1968–69) on the offensive line at guard, starting in both perfect seasons.

After moving to defense, Zapiec sat out most of the 1970 season as the result of an emergency appendectomy he underwent while on a road trip to Colorado for Penn State's second game that year. He returned in 1971 and emerged as an outstanding inside linebacker, making sixty-two tackles and intercepting four passes.

As an offensive lineman, he helped spring Bob Campbell for the game-winning two-point conversion in Penn State's 15–14 win over Kansas in the 1969 Orange Bowl. Earlier in the 1968 season, he recovered an onside kick to preserve a 28–24 victory over Army.

He played several years for Montreal in the Canadian Football League.

"He was tough, a really tough football player," Sandusky said.

John Skorupan (1972)

The Beaver, Pennsylvania, native continued the tradition, emerging as a starter as a sophomore in 1970 and finishing his career tied with Shane Conlan for fourth place with 274 tackles.

Skorupan made 106 tackles as a senior and also blocked three punts to receive All-America honors. Against Navy that season, he made seventeen tackles and returned an interception for a game-clinching touchdown.

He made nine interceptions in his career and went on to play eight seasons in the NFL with the Buffalo Bills and New York Giants.

"He was very athletic and lean," Sandusky said. "He was tough, but he was not real big."

Ed O'Neil (1973)

O'Neil, a native of Warren, Pennsylvania, made 126 tackles, the fourth-highest total in Penn State history, as a junior in his first season at linebacker after moving from defensive back. That season, he made twenty tackles in a win at Boston College.

As a senior in 1973, he had a solid season, making ten tackles against Stanford and returning an interception for a touchdown against Ohio University. He became only the second Penn State linebacker to be drafted in the first round. He played with the Detroit Lions for six seasons before finishing his career with the Green Bay Packers in 1980.

"I remember him coming as a defensive back and then he got bigger," Sandusky said. "He had great speed for a linebacker. He became very big. He grew tremendously over his four years."

Greg Buttle (1975)

A native of Linwood, New Jersey, Buttle holds Penn State records for tackles in a game, season, and career.

As a junior in 1974, he made twenty-four tackles against West Virginia, setting a record (later tied), and twenty-three against North Carolina State. He finished the year with a record 165 tackles, eighty-six solo and seventy-nine assisted.

As a senior he made 140 tackles and three interceptions. He finished his career with a record 343 tackles, far ahead of runner-up Brian Gelzheiser, who had 315. He finished his career by making thirteen tackles in a 13–6 loss to Alabama in the Sugar Bowl.

Buttle played nine seasons in the NFL with the New York Jets before he retired.

Greg Buttle holds Penn State records for tackles in a game, season, and career and played nine seasons in the NFL with the New York Jets.

"Confidence sticks out in my mind with Buttle," Sandusky said. "That won't ever change. He walked in wearing sunglasses and a swagger. He walked out the same way. He was a great leader and just so confident. He made others believe as he did."

Kurt Allerman (1976)

The Kinnelon, New Jersey, native emerged as a starter as a junior in 1975 and made eighty-seven tackles as a senior to lead Penn State. Allerman finished his career with 235 tackles, thirteenth on the Nittany Lions' all-time list. He finished his career by making sixteen tackles in a loss to Notre Dame in the Gator Bowl.

Allerman went on to play nine seasons in the NFL with the St. Louis Cardinals, Green Bay Packers, and Detroit Lions.

"He was really, really tough," Sandusky said. "He was a great person. He was mild mannered and quiet. On the field, he was as tough as anybody."

Shane Conlan (1985–86)

Conlan, a native of Frewsburg, New York, became Penn State's first All-America linebacker in nine years as a junior in 1985; he also earned All-America honors as a senior.

A converted defensive back and three-year starter, he made ninety-one tackles as a junior when Penn State went 11–0 in the regular season and lost to Oklahoma in the Orange Bowl. As a senior, he made a team-high seventy-nine tackles and led the Nittany Lions to a 12–0 season and the national championship.

Conlan capped his outstanding career in the Fiesta Bowl against Miami, making eight tackles and intercepting two passes, returning one 38 yards to set up the game-winning touchdown. He finished his career with 274 tackles, tied for fourth all time, a record 186 solo tackles, forty-one tackles for loss, and sixteen sacks.

He was drafted in the first round by the Buffalo Bills and was named the NFL Defensive Rookie of the Year in 1987. He played six years with the Bills, including three Super Bowls, and three years with the Los Angeles/St. Louis Rams.

"He had tremendous speed," Sandusky said. "He hit with such authority. He didn't just want to hit you; he wanted to stick you into the ground. He was the epitome of an old-fashioned football player. There was nothing fancy about him."

Andre Collins (1989)

A native of Cinnaminson, New Jersey, Collins played in the secondary at Penn State until moving to linebacker as a junior in 1988 when he led the Nittany Lions in tackles with 110.

As a senior he made 130 tackles, the third best in school history. He also blocked three punts, giving him four for his career and tying Ham's record for most in a season and career. He was one of five finalists for the Butkus Award in 1989.

Collins made 257 career tackles, seventh in Penn State history. He was drafted in the second round by Washington and played five seasons with the Redskins, three with the Cincinnati Bengals, and two with the Chicago Bears before retiring after the 1999 season.

"He had great speed and athleticism," Sandusky said. "He had a big smile and a lot of enthusiasm."

LaVar Arrington (1998-99)

Arrington joined Onkotz and Conlan as Penn State's only two-time All-America linebackers and the Nittany Lions' twelfth two-time All-America selection overall.

The Pittsburgh native became the first sophomore to be named the Big Ten Defensive Player of the Year in 1998. His highlight reel included a play in which he jumped over the Illinois offensive line to make a memorable tackle. In 1999 he had seventy-two tackles, twenty for loss, nine sacks, one interception, one forced fumble, two recoveries (one for a touchdown), and two blocked kicks.

That year, Arrington won the Butkus Award as the nation's top linebacker and the Bednarik Award as the nation's top defensive player. He also was a finalist for the Bronko Nagurski Trophy and the Lombardi Award.

Even though he started just two seasons and played just three, he ranks among Penn State's career leaders with nineteen sacks and thirty-nine tackles for loss. He's with the Washington Redskins, who drafted him with the second overall pick in the 2000 draft.

"He had just fantastic acceleration and jumping ability," Sandusky said. "He could cover ground quicker than anybody we've ever had."

LaVar Arrington won the Butkus Award as the nation's top linebacker and the Bednarik Award as the nation's top defensive player in 1999.

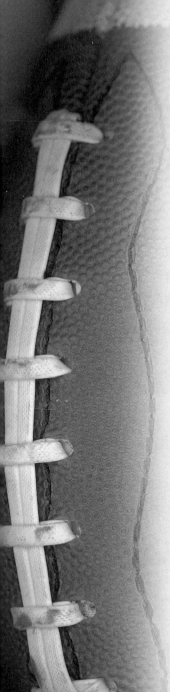

Sandusky Toys with Arrington

Former Penn State defensive coordinator Jerry Sandusky and former All-American linebacker LaVar Arrington have had a special relationship. Sandusky and Arrington both have outgoing, engaging, honest personalities and like to kid one another. Take their first meeting, for example.

Arrington, who had already committed to Penn State, was attending the Nittany Lions' football camp the summer before his senior year at North Hills High School. He was resting on the sideline with blisters on his heels when Sandusky saw one of Penn State's highest-profile recruits.

"I wasn't sure he was going to fit in that well here," Sandusky recalled. "I didn't know LaVar Arrington. He wasn't making many of the sessions at camp. He came up to me and said, 'Hey, am I going to start next year?'

"I looked at him. 'Well, LaVar, we usually start people who practice.' That wasn't exactly what he wanted to hear. . . . I thought he was totally filled up with himself. He's not like that at all. He's a very sensitive, caring person."

Arrington went on to become a two-time All-American, Penn State's first Butkus Award winner, the second pick in the 2000 NFL Draft, and a Pro Bowl linebacker with the Washington Redskins.

Brandon Short (1999)

Short, a native of McKeesport, Pennsylvania, is one of the few players to start four years at Penn State.

He started at defensive end as a freshman before moving to linebacker. He led the Nittany Lions in tackles as a junior and a senior. In 1999 he had 103 tackles, twelve for loss, four sacks, three pass break-ups, a fumble recovery, an interception, and a blocked kick.

He was a finalist for the Butkus Award and was named the defensive MVP of the Senior Bowl.

Short ranks sixth in Penn State history with 273 tackles and second with fifty-one tackles for loss. He was twice named to the All-Big Ten first team.

He plays for the New York Giants, who drafted him in the fourth round in 2000.

"He was intense," Sandusky said. "He had a determination to do something with his life in general. He had a lot of pride."

Perfect in Almost Every Way

T hey gathered in the huddle after each play and looked at each other quizzically. They couldn't figure out why the Kansas defense always seemed to have a free man.

The Penn State Nittany Lions were becoming increasingly frustrated as they tried to preserve their unbeaten season in the 1969 Orange Bowl. They trailed by seven points in the fourth quarter and couldn't generate offense.

"In the huddle everyone said, 'I blocked my man,'" halfback Charlie Pittman said. "We couldn't understand why the same guy kept making the tackle."

They would find out why a few minutes later. Chuck Burkhart completed a 47-yard pass to halfback Bob Campbell to the Kansas 3 and ran for a touchdown with fifteen seconds left, setting up one of the most bizarre finishes in college football history.

Penn State coach Joe Paterno decided to go for two points and the win. Hurried by 6'8" defensive end Vernon Venoy, Burkhart rushed his pass to Campbell in the back of the end zone and had it knocked away. The incompletion set off a wild celebration on the Kansas sideline and in the stands.

But an official standing in the back of the end zone waved his red penalty flag in the end zone; Kansas had twelve men on the field.

Quarterback Chuck Burkhart went 22–0 as a starter at Penn State and ran for a short touchdown in the 1969 Orange Bowl that set up a bizarre finish.

"One of the Kansas captains turned to me and said, 'What do you have?'" said umpire Foster Grose, the official who made the call. "'You have too many boys on the field.' When I said that, they all looked to one kid and he threw his hands to his head and dropped to his knees. They were all patting him on the back."

Given a second chance, the Lions scored the two points when Campbell ran off the left side, won 15–14, and capped their 11–0 season, their first perfect season since 1912. The memorable and improbable victory in the Orange Bowl came in the midst of their thirty-one-game unbeaten streak from 1967 to 1970, the longest in school history.

With back-to-back 11–0 seasons in 1968 and 1969, Penn State established itself as a national power and not a regional one and established Paterno, its brash head coach, as one of the brightest minds in the game.

"The Orange Bowl was the cap to a Cinderella season," Burkhart said. "We didn't know we were that good. I'm not sure the coaches thought we were that good. There wasn't a heck of a lot of pressure on the 1968 team. Penn State was never ranked that high before. I think we enjoyed the entire season. We probably didn't have as much fun in 1969."

The Lions were ranked second in the Associated Press poll and the third in the United Press International poll at the end of the 1968 season. They began the 1969 season with unprecedented expectations from their fans. They were ranked second, held on to beat twentieth-ranked Kansas State on the road and came from behind to edge Syracuse 15–14 on the road after trailing 14–0 in the fourth quarter.

"That was the sign of a great team," Paterno said of the win over the Orangemen.

The Lions finished the regular season unbeaten and went on to stop high-powered Missouri 10–3 in the Orange Bowl, a game in which they forced an astounding nine turnovers. But they wound up number two in the polls behind Texas after watching then-President Nixon present the Longhorns with a number one plaque before the bowl games were played.

Nixon's gesture in December caused a furor in Pennsylvania, but it didn't obscure Penn State's accomplishment. No other Nittany Lions teams posted back-to-back unbeaten, untied seasons before 1968 and 1969, or after. They were the first two of Paterno's five unbeaten teams.

"Sometimes that's the hardest part, to get the people to believe they can do it," Paterno said. "They'll always have a special place because they were the first."

Paterno planted the seeds for the unbeaten streak early in the 1967 season, his second year as head coach. Steve Smear, a defensive tackle, was the only sophomore who started in the season opener against Navy. He was joined by several of his classmates the next week.

After losing 23–22 to the Midshipmen, Paterno made a bold stroke that shaped Penn State for the next three seasons. The next game at Miami, he gradually inserted five other sophomores into the game with Smear: inside linebackers Dennis Onkotz and Jim Kates, outside linebacker Pete Johnson, cornerback Paul Johnson, and safety Neal Smith.

When defensive tackle Mike Reid returned in 1968 after knee surgery and linebacker Jack Ham started as a sophomore in 1968, they helped give Penn State as dominant a defense as Penn State has ever had. "So many of us started as sophomores," Onkotz said. "Playing together for three years is special. We got to know each other and count on each other. No one had to do more than their job."

A Presidential Snub

Penn State's unbeaten season in 1969 was hardly perfect. The Nittany Lions faced controversy twice late in the season, the first time because of a collective decision they made and the second time because of a decision a U.S. president made.

The Cotton Bowl and the Orange Bowl reportedly had Penn State as their top choices as the 7–0 Lions prepared to face Maryland in mid-November. One day after a 48–0 win over the Terrapins, the team held a meeting to vote on its bowl destination. Those were the days when bowl invitations were made a few games before the end of the regular season.

Ohio State was ranked number one and seemed headed to the Rose Bowl. Texas was number two and Penn State was ranked third. Paterno always has been in favor of the Lions playing the highest-ranked team available.

Some African-American players said they did not want to go to Dallas to play the Texas–Arkansas winner in the Cotton Bowl, but said they would go if the team voted to play there. It was six years after President Kennedy, a civil rights advocate, had been assassinated in Dallas. Other players complained about not being home for Christmas for the third year in a row.

"We had not been home for Christmas the two years before that," halfback Charlie Pittman said. "We thought we couldn't win the national championship. We didn't see why we should go to a bowl game, period."

Paterno went to the meeting carrying a schedule for the Cotton Bowl, expecting the Lions to vote that way. Several players also wanted to go to the Cotton Bowl, so there was much debate. Years later, offensive guard Charlie Zapiec called it an "open revolt." Defensive tackle Mike Reid called it "a disappointing set of circumstances."

Because they didn't have a shot at playing Ohio State and because they felt they couldn't win the national title by playing Texas or Arkansas, the Lions voted for a return trip to the Orange Bowl, where they would play Big Eight champion Missouri. Paterno also arranged for the team to practice in Fort Lauderdale, Florida, return home for a few days for Christmas, and then return to Miami for the game.

"All we did was practice at the Orange Bowl the year before," Zapiec said, "while Kansas went to the bowl parties and the beaches. We knew the ropes at the Orange Bowl and wanted to go back there."

"We got what we wanted," Pittman said.

Not exactly. When Michigan upset Ohio State a week later and Texas moved up to number one, the Lions were criticized for avoiding the best available team. "We thought if we couldn't win the national championship, let's go out and have fun," Zapiec said. "When Ohio State lost, we realized we had blown a chance at the national championship."

To make matters worse, President Richard Nixon announced that he would attend the Texas–Arkansas game on December 4 and would present the winner with a national championship trophy. ABC Sports commentator Bud Wilkinson, a former Oklahoma coach, was an official presidential advisor on physical fitness. He convinced Nixon to attend the game for political reasons.

After the Longhorns won 15–14, Nixon went to the locker room to proclaim Texas number one and present a plaque to coach Darrell Royal. Nixon, in an attempt to stem the growing resentment of Pennsylvanians and Republican Governor Raymond Shafer, announced that he would invite Paterno to the White House to present him with a plaque for Penn State having the nation's longest winning streak.

Paterno never heard Nixon because he clicked off his television when he saw Nixon walking to the Texas locker room. When a White House official called Paterno at home that night, he erupted. "You tell

(continued)

Halfback Charlie Pittman, Penn State's leading rusher from 1967 to 1969, voted with a majority of players to accept an invitation to the Orange Bowl instead of the Cotton Bowl after the 1969 season.

the president to take that trophy and shove it," Paterno said before hanging up the phone.

Penn State issued a statement from Paterno, which said: "It would seem to me to be a waste of his [Nixon's] very valuable time to present Penn State with a plaque for something it already indisputably owns."

Several years later, Paterno attended a dinner with Julie Nixon Eisenhower, the former president's daughter. The two chatted a while before the number one controversy came up. "It was unfortunate about the Watergate thing," Paterno said he told Nixon's daughter, "but some day he'll be remembered as a great president."

Nixon Eisenhower passed Paterno's remarks along to her father, who sent the coach a note thanking him for putting his daughter at ease. The former president and Paterno continued to write one another until Nixon's death.

Paterno might have forgiven Nixon for snubbing Penn State, but he has never forgotten it. The Lions went on to beat Missouri in the Orange Bowl to finish 11–0, but they finished second in the polls.

"It deprived some kids of the opportunity to be called national champions," Paterno said.

With one of the top defenses in the country, the offense wasn't asked to take many chances. Burkhart, who went 22–0 as the starter, passed the ball sparingly because the running game was so effective. Pittman, Campbell, Lydell Mitchell, Franco Harris, and Don Abbey provided speed, power, and depth in the backfield.

"The offense didn't turn it over," Pittman said. "We never put ourselves in a position to lose."

Penn State had strong leadership in those years from Reid and Smear on defense and from Pittman and linemen John Kulka and Tom Jackson on offense. Off the field they policed one another and maintained order. On the field they exuded confidence, even though the Lions had made only periodic appearances in the top ten until then. "Those teams did not know how to lose," linebacker Gary Gray said. "Guys went into every game expecting to win. They didn't even consider losing."

Nine players from those teams were chosen as first-team All-Americans and six played in the NFL for at least five years. Ham, Kwalick, Onkotz, and Reid are in the College Football Hall of Fame, and Ham and Harris are in the Pro Football Hall of Fame.

Many of the players on those teams, though, say they won because of their intelligence and preparedness.

"I don't think a lot of people we had were outstanding," Campbell said, "but we had a lot of people who had outstanding games. Certain people had great games when we needed them."

Penn State began the 1968 season ranked tenth in the nation, moving up to number three with home wins over Navy and Kansas State and a road victory at West Virginia. That set up a nationally televised game at UCLA, which had beaten the

Lions in their last four meetings, two of which were draped in controversy.

In 1965 the Bruins won 24–22 at Beaver Stadium and UCLA assistant coach Pepper Rodgers was accused of calling the plays and directing Gary Beban over a two-way radio from the press box to the field. Head coach Tommy Prothro denied ordering or knowing about the radio.

In 1966 Paterno's first season as head coach, Penn State went to Los Angeles to take on the third-ranked Bruins and lost 49–11. But Prothro angered Paterno when he ordered an onside kick with thirty-eight seconds left and UCLA ahead 42–11. The Lions returned to Los Angeles two years later with more experience and more resolve.

"Deep down, I remembered [what Prothro had done]," Paterno said. "But I also felt that because UCLA was playing so well over time, we really wanted to win out there. We went out there with things to prove."

With the game scoreless in the second quarter, five Penn State players broke through UCLA's punt protection. Ham blocked the kick, and Kates picked it up and ran 36 yards for a touchdown. The Lions, who never trailed, scored two second-half touchdowns to win 21–6.

"That was one of my better games," Kates said. "It was a big game because they beat us the year before [17–15] on a similar play. It was a TV game and we always liked to play on TV."

Back in State College, about 2,000 students celebrated on College Avenue, rocking buses and cars. A throng of students and the Blue Band met the Lions at 5:00 A.M. at the Rec Hall on their return to campus. Penn State surprisingly dropped to number four in the rankings, but it was clear the Lions were contenders for the national championship. They had only one more scare in the regular season, which came two weeks after the UCLA win.

Penn State faced Army, which had gone 9–3 against the Lions since Paterno became an assistant coach in 1950, including three for three at Beaver Stadium. Penn State led the entire game, but the Cadets cut the lead to 22–17 with two and a half minutes left. Army tried an onside kick and the football disappeared in a pile of players.

Suddenly, the ball squirted into the hands of Kwalick, the All-America tight end, who returned it 53 yards for a touchdown. Army scored again and tried another onside kick, but Charlie Zapiec fell on it to preserve the Lions' 28–24 win. "I remember it as if it was yesterday," Kwalick said. "It is amazing that one of the first things Penn Staters say to me is that they remember that onside kick in the Army game."

The Lions rolled the rest of the way, beating Miami, Maryland, Pittsburgh, and Syracuse. Two days after the 48–0 romp over the Terrapins, Penn State accepted an invitation to play Kansas in the Orange Bowl in Miami. The game against the Orangemen had been pushed back to December 7 to accommodate ABC for a national telecast.

Campbell, a senior, had missed a few games earlier in the season with a separated shoulder. He had returned to the lineup and looked forward to facing Syracuse because he had grown up in upstate New York. He carried twenty-four times for two touchdowns and 239 yards, 11 yards shy of what was then the school record.

Campbell scored on an 87-yard run in the second quarter, Penn State's longest in seventy-six years, in the Lions' 30–12 victory. In the fourth quarter he ran over a former high school opponent for an 18-yard touchdown and chucked the ball into the north stands. A miffed Paterno told him he had to pay for

Ted Kwalick, a two-time All-America tight end, returned an onside kick for a touchdown against Army in 1968 that kept alive the Nittany Lions' unbeaten streak.

the ball and benched him the rest of the game. "Penn State–Syracuse was bigger than Penn State–Pittsburgh at that time," Campbell said. "We just had a good game. Everything went well, except that I had to pay for the ball."

The third-ranked Lions were making their first appearance in a New Year's Day bowl game since 1947. Number six Kansas was making its first bowl appearance anywhere since 1947. The once-beaten Jayhawks had the highest-scoring offense in the country with Bobby Douglass at quarterback and John Riggins at fullback.

Penn State had its most prolific offense since 1916, but the game turned out to be a defensive struggle. The Lions committed four turnovers in the first half after making just fourteen all season, yet they tied it 7–7 at the half on Pittman's 13-yard run. In the second half they drove to the Kansas 1, but Pittman was thrown for a 2-yard loss on fourth down.

Kansas took a 14–7 lead early in the fourth quarter and was in position to put it away. The Jayhawks faced fourth and 1 at the Penn State 5 with ten minutes left and passed up a short field goal try to go for it. The 235-pound Riggins tried the right side and thundered toward 215-pound linebacker Pete Johnson. But Johnson hit him low and cornerback Paul Johnson (no relation) hit him high, stopping Riggins short of a first down.

"Riggins was on me almost instantly," Pete Johnson said. "I remember seeing this big thigh and smacking into it. I was surprised he was moving sideways and that he went down so easily."

It stayed 14–7 until Reid sacked Douglass twice and Neal Smith partially blocked a Kansas punt. The ball bounced out of bounds at the 50 with 1:16 left. On the sideline Paterno told Burkhart to throw a deep pass over Campbell's head to set up short passes to Kwalick. But in the huddle Campbell had something else in mind.

"I told Chuck to throw it right for the goalpost for me," Campbell said. "He threw it as far as he could. I caught it and that was the name of that tune."

"Bob said, 'I'm going to get open,' " Burkhart said. "I said, 'If you get open, I'll get you the ball.' "

Campbell hauled it in at the 20 and took it to the 3. From there Kansas twice stopped fullback Tom Cherry for no gain before Paterno sent in a "scissors" play for Pittman off the left side. But the Jayhawks were keying on Pittman and Burkhart realized it when he stepped to the line.

He faked a handoff to Pittman, kept the ball, and ran around left end for the first touchdown of his career with eight seconds left. Pittman thought he had fumbled. "Charlie would have been tackled on the spot," Burkhart said. "Kansas had penetrated, so I just took off."

Paterno quickly decided to go for two points and the win. He sent in a play that sent Campbell to the back of the end zone and Kwalick to the goal line and gave Burkhart the option to pass or run. Burkhart faced heavy pressure on his rollout and tried to throw to Campbell, but it was broken up.

Kansas fans poured out of the stands to join the players in celebration, but Grose waved his red flag. In the confusion after Burkhart's pass to Campbell, the Jayhawks left twelve men on the field for Penn State's final series. "I think only a few of us recognized that twelve men were on the field," Pete Johnson said. "I think there were a few plays when they had thirteen guys on the field. It was almost like it was fated to happen."

After the ball was moved 1½ yards from the goal line, Campbell ran to the left and dove into the end zone to give

Penn State a crazy 15–14 victory, the first by an Eastern school in the Orange Bowl since 1937.

"The only thing in sports that has come close to it was the Stanford–California game [in 1982]," Pittman said. "It has to be one of the most fantastic finishes in college sports. Sad tears turned to happy tears. It was just unbelievable."

The Nittany Lions finished with the most wins (eleven) and highest ranking (second in the poll) in school history. They wound up behind Ohio State, which entered the post-season ranked number one and won the national championship by defeating USC in the Rose Bowl.

In the off-season Paterno had turned down an offer from the Pittsburgh Steelers to become their head coach. More attention was being focused on Penn State, which began the 1969 season with great expectations, a number two ranking, and fifteen returning starters, including ten on defense.

The Lions easily beat Navy and Colorado in their first two games before they faced their first ranked opponent, number twenty Kansas State, on the road. Penn State forced four turnovers in the first half and took a 17–0 lead in the third quarter before holding on to win 17–14. Offensive tackle Vic Surma recovered an onside kick for the Lions with fifteen seconds to go.

The Lions' unbeaten streak was in further jeopardy two weeks later at Syracuse. The Orangemen used outstanding punt returns by Greg Allen to go up 14–0 at the half. The lead could have been larger, but cornerback George Landis blocked two field goals and Allen fell down in the backfield on fourth and 2 from the Penn State 3 late in the second quarter.

"If we'd come in down 17–0 or 21–0, it might have been different," Paterno said. "We felt we could win if we stopped horsing around."

Defensive tackle Mike Reid (68) won the Outland Trophy in 1969 as the nation's outstanding interior lineman and is one of four Penn State players from the 1968 and 1969 teams to be inducted into the College Football Hall of Fame.

Penn State failed to score after Landis recovered a fumble at the Syracuse 12 in the third quarter. The Orangemen held the Lions scoreless until the fourth quarter when Ham recovered Allen's fumble at the Syracuse 32. On fourth down from the 15, the Orangemen were penalized for pass interference, which enabled Mitchell to score on the next play.

On a play reminiscent of the Orange Bowl win over Kansas, Harris caught a pass and was stopped at the 1 on a two-point conversion try. But Syracuse was penalized for holding, which enabled Harris to run for the two points to make it 14–8.

After John Ebersole partially blocked a punt, Penn State took over at the Syracuse 39. Harris bolted 36 yards on second down for the tie and Mike Reitz kicked the extra point for a

15–14 lead with about seven minutes to go. Neither team scored again, but Syracuse coach Ben Schwartzwalder complained about poor officiating at a press luncheon two days later. At least one Lion seemed almost to agree. "That was a game we certainly didn't deserve to win," Reid said. "Syracuse rose to a marvelous level that afternoon and we figured out a way to win."

As the season unfolded Penn State remained unbeaten playing what its critics perceived to be a weak schedule. Two days after pulverizing Maryland 48–0, the Lions accepted an invitation to play in the Orange Bowl for the second year in a row after much discussion.

In the Orange Bowl Penn State manhandled sixth-ranked Missouri 10–3, reducing one of the nation's most explosive teams to rubble. The Nittany Lions intercepted seven passes, an all-time major bowl record, recovered two fumbles, and held 1,300-yard rusher Joe Moore to 36 yards.

Penn State scored its points in a twenty-one-second span in the first quarter. Reitz kicked a 29-yard field goal before Reid forced Moore to fumble on the kickoff, which was recovered by Mike Smith. On the next play Burkhart threw a short pass to Mitchell, who eluded a tackler and scored on a 28-yard play.

The Tigers kicked a field goal late in the second quarter, but they never scored again, despite threatening several times. Landis made his second interception of the game at the goal line with twenty-two seconds left to seal back-to-back Orange Bowl wins and 11–0 seasons for the Lions.

"When we went on the field [for Missouri's final series], Mike Reid said, 'They're not going to score,'" according to Landis. "He said it very loudly and very forcefully. That's the mentality we had. We had a lot of pride."

Penn State, however, had to settle for being number two again. Texas beat Notre Dame in the Cotton Bowl to win the national championship. "I don't think people gave that team enough credit for holding down Missouri," Paterno said. "To hold them to three points was a fantastic effort."

The Lions' unbeaten streak went to thirty-one games before Colorado routed them 41–13 in the second game of the 1970 season. But the 1968 and 1969 teams put Penn State among college football's elite and paved the way for a decade of unparalleled success. The Lions won at least ten games six times in the 1970s and made three trips to the Sugar Bowl, two to the Cotton, and one to the Orange.

"They seemed to be much more mature than most teams I've had," Paterno said of his 1968 and 1969 teams. "I don't think I've ever felt that we were going to lose a game."

A Brother's Tribute

At the end of spring practice in 1971, Penn State coach Joe Paterno met with a promising sophomore running back from suburban Philadelphia. John Cappelletti didn't know what to expect, but he quickly found out what Paterno wanted.

"We're loaded up at running back," Paterno said then. "We need defensive backs. We think you can play the position and maybe you can go back to running back later."

Cappelletti didn't argue; he played in the Nittany Lions' secondary that season while Lydell Mitchell and Franco Harris combined to give Penn State a devastating rushing attack. A year later, when Mitchell and Harris were off to the NFL, he returned to offense and rushed for 1,117 yards.

Two years later as a senior, Cappelletti powered his way to 1,522 yards and led the Lions to a 12–0 season and a win in the Orange Bowl. He beat the odds and won the 1973 Heisman Trophy, offering a memorable acceptance speech.

"He was tremendous, just a workhorse," said Tom Shuman, the quarterback on Penn State's 1973 team. "He was very shifty and sneaky fast. He just had an ability to stay on his feet. He was incredible."

The 6'1", 225-pound Cappelletti ranks ninth in Penn State history with 2,639 career rushing yards, but he's the only player among the top fifteen who ran the ball just two seasons. When he moved back to offense in 1972, he underwent a bumpy transition.

John Cappelletti rushed for 1,522 yards in 1973, led Penn State to a 12–0 season, and became the Nittany Lions' only Heisman Trophy winner.

"I actually felt uncomfortable when I went back to offense," he said. "It took me awhile to start to feel comfortable. It was the first time I played running back at that level. I had a hard time when I was getting hit. I was too concerned about the ball. Not having practiced on offense did have an effect.

"I really had only one goal, to get better and better every week. I did not want to slide backwards. It was a relatively simple process for me."

Cappelletti's formula helped him win the Heisman, but it couldn't help Penn State win the national championship. The Lions went undefeated against a schedule that included Stanford, Iowa, Maryland, North Carolina State, and Louisiana State, but they finished fifth in the polls behind national champion Notre Dame and some teams that had ties.

"Obviously we were very disappointed and frustrated," Shuman said, "from the standpoint that we felt we weren't given a shot to prove what we could do. We felt we were every bit as good as Notre Dame or Alabama and we didn't get a chance to play them."

A year earlier, Cappelletti struggled early with a leg injury until he rushed for 124 yards in a 35–17 victory at Illinois. He went on to post four more 100-yard games and helped Penn State go 10–1 in the regular season and gain an invitation to the Sugar Bowl against second-ranked Oklahoma.

But the night before the game, Cappelletti contracted a viral infection and had a temperature of 102 degrees. Without him, the Lions mustered just 196 total yards, including 49 on the ground, and lost four fumbles. The Sooners won 14–0, even though they lost five fumbles.

"I had practiced all week," Cappelletti recalled. "I still had my tonsils in at that time and sometimes tonsils collect infections. I had a real bad case of whatever it was. Once I had my tonsils out a few years later, I never felt that way again."

Penn State entered the 1973 season with high hopes and were ranked seventh in the Associated Press poll. The Lions returned several veterans on defense, including tackle Randy Crowder and linebacker Ed O'Neil, and nine of eleven starters on offense.

Cappelletti was going to run behind an experienced offensive line that started Dan Natale at tight end, Charlie Getty and Ron LaPorta at tackle, Mark Markovich and John Nessel at guard, and Jack Baiorunos at center. "Cappy got better and better every week," said Shuman, then in his first season as the starting quarterback. "He had some horses in front of him as well. Everybody came together and jelled. We became better and better as a team. I'm not sure anybody could have beaten us."

Penn State opened the season at Stanford, where the Lions and Cappelletti got off to a so-so start in a 20–6 win. He fumbled twice and gained just 76 yards on twenty-six carries. He ran for 104 yards and a touchdown in a 39–0 romp over Navy and had 88 yards and one score in a 27–8 victory over Iowa.

Three games into his senior season, Cappelletti was averaging less than 90 yards a game and not exactly creating a stir across the country. That would change the following week at Air Force, where the Falcons were 2–0. Not bothered by the high altitude of Colorado Springs, Cappelletti carried thirty-four times for 187 yards and two touchdowns.

Against Army, he rushed seventeen times for 151 yards, including a career-best 60-yard run, in a 54–3 beating. The passing game also was improving with Shuman on his way to throwing for 1,375 yards and thirteen touchdowns against just five interceptions. John Hufnagel had thrown for 2,039 yards the year before as a senior, so no one knew what to expect from Shuman.

"I don't know if Joe ever had a balanced offense," Cappelletti said. "It was run and play defense in those days. John and Tom brought different things that helped the running game. John was a decent dropback passer, but he was excellent outside the pocket. If something was not there, he was gone. That threat helped the running game.

"Tommy was a little bit different. He was a dropback passer with a good, strong arm. We had good wide receivers that year [Gary Hayman and Chuck Herd]."

Cappelletti suffered a slight shoulder injury and served as a decoy the next week against Syracuse, where he started and quickly left. It was the only game in Penn State's last eight in the regular season that he would not gain 100 yards or more.

Cappelletti cemented his place in Penn State and college football history over the next five games. The Lions routed West Virginia 62–14 after the Mountaineers had opened the season ranked in the top twenty. Cappelletti carried twenty-four times and plowed his way for 130 yards and a career-high four touchdowns, igniting the talk of him as a Heisman Trophy candidate. "I remembered the West Virginia game the most from that year," Shuman said. "If there was one game when he just took over and dominated, that was it. He just amazed me with the runs he made that day."

The next week, Cappelletti rushed a school-record thirty-seven times for 202 yards against Maryland, which had one of the best run defenses in the nation. The Terrapins tied it 22–22 before halftime before Cappelletti took over in the second half in Penn State's 42–22 victory.

"I remember him sitting in the training room after games with ice packs all over his body," Natale said. "His arms and legs were black and blue. He took a beating. He would take you on and gained a lot of yards after the first contact."

"I was running the ball an awful lot," Cappelletti said. "Every time I touched the ball, I was hit once or twice before I went down. I got hit a lot. I generally wasn't going to go down on the first hit unless somebody got penetration. My games were measured sometimes in how much ice I put on."

Penn State faced North Carolina State the next week, a team that had battled the Lions the previous year. The Wolfpack had a powerful offense that featured twins Dave and Don Buckey and a brash coach named Lou Holtz.

In blustery weather NC State took a 14–9 halftime lead, scoring the first rushing touchdowns of the season against the Lions. Penn State rebounded quickly in the third quarter and took a 22–14 lead on Cappelletti's 20-yard run and Hayman's 80-yard punt return. The Wolfpack tied it at twenty-two and then again at twenty-nine after the Lions had scored again.

Cappelletti scored on a 27-yard run in the middle of the fourth quarter before Penn State held on to win 35–29. He finished with a school-record forty-one carries for a career-high 220 yards and three touchdowns.

"That game went back and forth," Natale said. "I remember Cappy's run in the fourth quarter. I was on the ground and I looked up and he was in the end zone."

"We didn't have a sense of how good they were," Cappelletti said. "Once we got into the game, we knew. They'd score and we'd score. We scored one more time to make the difference."

The Heisman talk intensified after the NC State game and gained even more momentum when Cappelletti rushed for 204 yards and four touchdowns in a 49–10 thrashing of Ohio University. His third straight 200-yard game set a school record for consecutive games, most in one season and most in a career.

Cappelletti was barely mentioned as an All-America candidate before the season. Now he was the leading candidate for the Heisman and was even being touted by Penn State. "It started around midseason," Cappelletti said. "When I started to string those games together, it really picked up."

That week, sixth-ranked Penn State accepted an invitation to play seventh-ranked LSU in the Orange Bowl. Number one Alabama accepted an offer to face number three Notre Dame in the Sugar Bowl. The Lions appeared to be out of the running for a national championship, unless the Crimson Tide or the Fighting Irish lost. But neither did.

Johnny Majors brought Pitt's best team in years into Beaver Stadium for the season finale, and the Panthers surprised the lethargic Lions with a 13–3 halftime lead. Tony Dorsett, then a freshman and one of the leading rushers in the nation, ran for a touchdown.

"We were in trouble that game," Shuman recalled. "We were a little disappointed in ourselves at halftime and Joe was a little frustrated with us that day."

Penn State, perhaps inspired by Paterno's halftime talk or incensed when Pitt kicker Carson Long shook his fist at the Lions' bench after kicking a field goal right before the half, dominated the second half. The Lions snapped the ball five times from inside the 10 before backup Bob Nagle scored.

Cappelletti gave Penn State the lead for good in the fourth quarter with a short run, and the Lions went on to win 35–13 and finish 11–0 in the regular season. He finished with 161 yards on thirty-seven carries against the Panthers and seemed to solidify his Heisman campaign.

John Cappelletti posted three straight 200-yard games against Maryland, North Carolina State, and Ohio University in November 1973.

Linebacker Ed O'Neil (87) was one of Penn State's leaders on defense in 1973 and was named to three All-America teams.

Within the next few weeks, Cappelletti was selected a consensus All-American. Crowder and O'Neil also were named to All-America first teams. Getty, Markovich, and Natale were named to the second team.

Cappelletti easily won the Heisman Trophy over Ohio State offensive tackle John Hicks and also the Maxwell Award as the nation's outstanding player. In those days the Heisman winner was announced in a press release without a television show. Cappelletti received word that he had won while taping a Bob Hope Christmas show with the rest of the Associated Press All-America team. "We were in a TV studio in New York," he said. "Somebody from the Heisman committee came up to me and told me I won. That was pretty much it."

Cappelletti attended several events over the next week and barely contemplated his acceptance speech. "In between dozens of events there, I started to think what I was gonna say," he said. "There was the main part of the speech. Then I wrote it on the bottom of my notes. I just put 'Joey' down there. I wasn't sure what exactly was gonna happen. I didn't know how much I'd elaborate.

"Nobody knew. I wasn't positive how it was gonna come out."

Cappelletti offered the most memorable acceptance speech in the history of the Heisman. After thanking his family, his high school coach, Paterno, his teammates, and Penn State backfield coach Bob Phillips, he paused to recognize his eleven-year-old brother, Joey, who was stricken with leukemia.

"The youngest member of my family, Joseph, is very ill," Cappelletti said. "He has leukemia. If I can dedicate this trophy to him tonight and give him a couple days of happiness, this is worth everything. I think a lot of people think that I go through a lot on Saturdays and during the week as most athletes do, and you get your bumps and bruises and it is a terrific battle out there on the field.

"Only for me it is on Saturdays and it's only in the fall. For Joseph it is all year-round and it is a battle that is unending with him and he puts up with much more than I'll ever put up with. And I think this trophy is more his than mine because he has been a great inspiration to me."

Cappelletti was the best player on the team and perhaps the most respected.

"We knew his brother was sick," Natale said. "That showed you what kind of guy he was. It showed his upbringing. He was unselfish. It couldn't have happened to a nicer guy."

"John was always a very humble individual," Shuman said, "and a very modest individual. He gave a great deal of credit to his offensive line."

After Joey Cappelletti died in 1976, John wrote a book titled *Something for Joey* that was made into a television movie in 1977. The book remains in circulation and still draws response. "A lot of fourth- and fifth-graders read that book and send me packets of notes," Cappelletti said. "It still has value today. I can see it in their comments. 'I want to be a better brother. I want to be a better son.' It spurs them on to think about their lives."

Cappelletti still had one more game to play for Penn State following the Heisman presentation. The number six Nittany Lions were one of only three unbeaten and untied teams in the country. Alabama and Notre Dame, the other two, ranked number one and number three respectively, were meeting in the Sugar Bowl.

Penn State's chances of moving past other teams in the polls were hurt when their bowl opponent LSU lost to

Alabama and Tulane after accepting the Orange Bowl berth and dropping to thirteenth in the polls.

Notre Dame beat Alabama 24–23 in the Sugar Bowl on New Year's Eve in Ara Parseghian's final game as Irish coach, so the Lions knew they had no shot when they took the field the next night in Miami.

Penn State started slowly and fell behind 7–0 before going ahead on Chris Bahr's 44-yard field goal and Shuman's 72-yard pass to Herd. The Lions took a 16–7 halftime lead on Cappelletti's short run, but he struggled. The Tigers held him to 50 yards on twenty-six carries in wet weather, the worst outing of his career. "Charley McClendon had LSU ready to play," Natale said. "They did a great job on Cappy. It was a tough, tough game. Not playing in the Sugar Bowl was something we couldn't control."

The Lions became the first team in school history to go 12–0, but they finished fifth in both major polls. After the game, Paterno, frustrated that his undefeated teams in 1968 and 1969 also were snubbed, said Penn State had finished number one in the "Paterno Poll." He later bought commemorative rings for the players.

"I was pleasantly surprised that Joe stepped up and named us number one in his poll," Cappelletti said. "That was a little out of character for him. He said, 'This team right here could have played with anybody. This is not a fair system.' No matter what we did, we were not going to get the recognition."

John Cappelletti received the recognition he deserved. He went on to be drafted in the first round by the Los Angeles Rams and played ten seasons in the NFL with the Rams and the San Diego Chargers. He was inducted into the College Football Hall of Fame in 1993.

"I started to get a sense of the tailback tradition of Penn State when I was there," he said. "I watched Lydell carry the load his senior year. He had a phenomenal year. He gave me something to shoot for. He set a standard for me.

"One of my goals was to have the best year [by a running back] in Penn State history."

John Cappelletti didn't have the best year, but he had the most memorable one.

Lions Catch Nebraska: A National Title

M ike McCloskey never lived in Nebraska or played
football for the Cornhuskers, but he remains a well-
known figure for thousands in that state.

A few years ago, McCloskey was invited to Father
Flanagan's Boys Town in Omaha to speak at a banquet, where
hundreds of Cornhuskers fans remembered his place in
Nebraska lore. A former tight end for Penn State, McCloskey
made a controversial catch on the sideline that set up the
winning touchdown in the Nittany Lions' thrilling 27–24 win
over the Cornhuskers in 1982.

After videotape of his catch was shown at the banquet,
McCloskey decided to have some fun.

"Ah, I feel guilty," he told the audience. "I can't take it
anymore. I was out of bounds."

The next morning, a headline in an Omaha newspaper
blared: "Penn State Tight End Comes Clean." The game
between the second-ranked Cornhuskers and the eighth-
ranked Nittany Lions remains arguably the greatest game
played at Beaver Stadium and probably the most controversial

one. It propelled Penn State to its first national championship and cost Nebraska a shot at the national title.

Penn State came from behind in the final seventy-eight seconds with a 65-yard drive that featured McCloskey's catch at the 2 yard line and backup tight end Kirk Bowman's touchdown with four seconds left.

"It's truly amazing the number of people who not only remember it, but remember it vividly," McCloskey said. "It's kind of my fifteen seconds of fame. If I had caught it clearly inbounds, it probably wouldn't be remembered. The thing had a life of its own and that surprised me."

Bowman, who never played tight end until that season, caught two touchdown passes that afternoon, the first two of his career. A week earlier against Rutgers, he had dropped a sure touchdown pass in the end zone, prompting teammates to call him "Stonehands."

"That's my fifteen minutes of fame that I keep living," Bowman said. "That Nebraska game will always hold a special place for me. What happened in that game is every kid's dream."

Bowman started following the Nittany Lions as a child. He and his father, Wayne, a former Penn State offensive lineman in the 1960s, used to drive to State College two or three Saturdays each fall. Those were the days when the Bowmans sat in the bleachers in the south end zone and when kids were allowed on the field after the game to meet their heroes. Kirk still has a chinstrap he received from John Cappelletti, Penn State's only Heisman Trophy winner.

Kirk took greater satisfaction from the Nebraska game because his father, who ended his Penn State football career in order to help raise Kirk and work full-time to support his family, saw the game in person. "That game means something completely different to me," he said, "than to other people."

It remains one of the most significant games in Penn State history. By 1982 coach Joe Paterno's pursuit of a national championship had become a cruel joke. The Nittany Lions had gone unbeaten in the regular season four times in the previous fourteen years without winning a national title. In three of those years, they won the Orange Bowl and twice finished second in the polls and once fifth.

In 1981 Penn State had reached number one in the polls before losing to Miami and Alabama. But after opening the 1982 season with three easy wins, the Lions faced a team that seemingly had All-Americans everywhere: Turner Gill at quarterback, Mike Rozier and Roger Craig in the backfield, Irving Fryar at flanker, and Dave Rimington and Dean Steinkuhler on the offensive line.

"If anything occurred during that game, it was just realizing that we—Penn State players and fans—could get over the hump on the national championship thing," Bowman said. "I think it was the first game that we thought, 'Maybe we could do this.'"

Nebraska was a juggernaut, rolling up a staggering 883 yards and forty-three first downs in a 68–0 win over New Mexico State the previous week. Because of Nebraska's reputation and because it was the first game under the lights at Beaver Stadium, a buzz filled the air in anticipation.

Back then, Penn State players dressed at the locker room next to their practice field and rode on buses to the stadium. Almost twenty-five years later, McCloskey remembers that ride in great detail. "The crowd was crazy," he said. "It was warm and you could see the [temporary] lights lighting up the stadium. People were lining the road just waiting for the buses to come up. It was like they wanted blood."

The Lions did not disappoint their fans. After Todd Blackledge threw touchdown passes to Kenny Jackson and

Chemistry Class

Penn State ended its 96-year quest by beating Georgia 27–23 in the Sugar Bowl for the 1982 national championship. But some players on the 1982 team and some observers thought the Nittany Lions were even better the year before.

Penn State went 10–2 in 1981, beating Nebraska, Notre Dame, top-ranked Pittsburgh, and Southern California in the Fiesta Bowl and losing to Miami and Alabama. Eleven starters from that team moved on, including offensive guards Mike Munchak and Sean Farrell, both taken in the first round of the NFL Draft.

"Quite honestly, we had a more talented team in '81," said Todd Blackledge, quarterback of both teams. "We had a more dominating offensive line with Munchak and Farrell. We were better and more phys-ical on defense. We just didn't have the same chemistry."

With just eleven returning starters in 1982, the Nittany Lions opened 4–0, including a thrilling win over Nebraska, lost to Alabama 42–21 and reeled off seven straight wins to win the school's first national title.

"The leadership was a little better in '82," Blackledge said. "There was just a different spirit to that team."

Gregg Garrity that were wiped out by penalties, tailback Curt Warner made a pretty over-the-shoulder catch for 43 yards. That set up Blackledge's 14-yard touchdown pass to Bowman.

On the play Penn State had lined up in its short-yardage formation with three running backs and two tight ends, Bowman and McCloskey. That week, though, the coaches felt that the strong-side tight end would get open, so they moved McCloskey to the strong side and Bowman to the weak side.

The coaches guessed wrong. Bowman was wide open when Blackledge hit him. He also would be alone with the game on the line in the fourth quarter.

"It's kind of interesting," Bowman said. "They were the only two times we ran it and the only two times we swapped sides in that formation. Let's face it. They usually brought me in so they could run my way. I was not known for my pass-catching prowess."

Warner put Penn State up 14–0 with a 2-yard run in the second quarter, but he missed most of the second half with leg cramps. The Lions continued to move the ball, but freshman Massimo Manca missed three field goals. The defense kept Nebraska and its powerful arsenal scoreless until late in the first half.

"I remember feeling like every play had this vital importance to it," said linebacker Scott Radecic. "There are some games you play when you think you have the other team backed up. 'Nothing's really going to happen this series.' But playing Nebraska, they had the ability to score on every play."

The Cornhuskers finally scored when Gill threw a 30-yard touchdown pass to Fryar to make it 14–7 at the half, a half in which the Lions had their way everywhere except on the scoreboard. "We dominated the game in the first half," Blackledge

*Todd Blackledge passed for three touchdowns in Penn State's thrilling
27–24 win over Nebraska in 1982.*

said. "We should have been way out in front. To their credit, they battled back. They were a great team."

Blackledge opened the second half with an 18-yard touchdown pass to Jackson, capping an 83-yard drive for a 21–7 lead. Nebraska responded behind Gill and Rozier, the 1983 Heisman winner, who caught a short swing pass for a touchdown.

In the fourth quarter Blackledge threw what he and the Lions thought was an incomplete screen pass. But the officials ruled that it was a lateral and a fumble, which the Cornhuskers recovered to set up a field goal that made it 21–17.

"We never felt panicked," Radecic said. "We had such an explosive offense. We knew if we could keep it close and could put the ball back in our offense's hands, they could score."

The Penn State offense, however, stalled again, giving Nebraska a chance to take the lead. Gill directed an 80-yard drive and ended it with a 1-yard dive into the end zone, putting the Cornhuskers ahead for the first time at 24–21 with just 1:18 to go.

That set the stage for one of the greatest finishes in Penn State history. Nebraska's kickoff sailed into the end zone for a touchback, but the Cornhuskers' Dave Ridder pushed a Lion to the ground after the whistle had blown. The 15-yard personal foul penalty allowed Penn State to start from its 35, but with no timeouts left.

Blackledge jogged onto the field and into the huddle full of confidence. He was on his way to completing twenty-three of thirty-nine passes for 295 yards and three touchdowns. He also was thinking of one of his favorite Bible passages, Philippians 4:13, which reads: "I have the strength for everything through Him who empowers me."

"I had a deep belief that we were going to win the game," Blackledge said two decades later, "that we had played well enough to win. Not that God chooses sides in a football game,

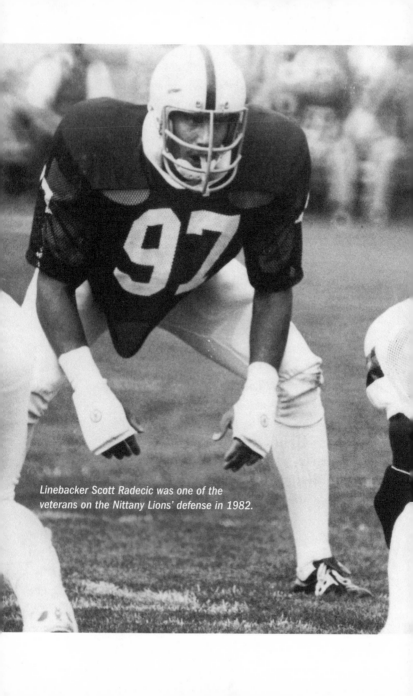

Linebacker Scott Radecic was one of the veterans on the Nittany Lions' defense in 1982.

but I had supreme confidence we would win. I didn't say that to the rest of the guys, but I guess it was on my face, in my eyes, and in my voice that we were gonna get it done."

"Todd Blackledge got in the huddle and he was calm, cool, and collected," Bowman said. "He said, 'We practice this every day. We're gonna march down the field and score.' There was calmness and no panic."

Blackledge threw a screen pass to Skeeter Nichols for 16 yards to open the drive. After an incompletion, he found Jackson for another 16 yards to the Nebraska 33. Then Blackledge tried to surprise the Cornhuskers, calling a draw play to Jonathan Williams, who was thrown for a 1-yard loss.

Two incompletions set up fourth and 11 at the 34. Paterno considered trying a tying field goal, but Manca had struggled. So the Lions went for the first down and got it when Blackledge hit Jackson on a curl pattern for 11 yards.

"I'll never forget that last drive," Garrity said. "We had to score to win. It seemed like there was no panic in the huddle. For some reason we had the confidence against a great Nebraska team that we could do it."

Twenty-seven seconds remained as the frenzied crowd became louder and the Lions hurried to the line. Blackledge dropped back, saw no receiver open, and took off, running out of bounds at the 17 with thirteen seconds left. One of the most memorable plays in Penn State and Nebraska history followed.

McCloskey lined up on the left side and ran an out pattern to the Penn State sideline on the near side of the field. Blackledge led him more than he needed to lead him and McCloskey pulled it in, dragging his feet across the sideline.

Radecic, who was standing on the sideline, contends the catch was good; Blackledge and Garrity say they thought

McCloskey was out of bounds; and McCloskey and Bowman say it was too close to call.

The side judge ruled that McCloskey had made the catch before he stepped out of bounds at the 2, despite the animated protests of Nebraska players.

"Depending on how you look at it, at what angle, at what speed the videotape is playing, it looks different almost every time," McCloskey said. "It's a bang-bang play for the referee. The Nebraska people clearly view it as being out of bounds. I understand that."

"McCloskey was dragging his feet and the ref was looking down," Garrity said. "He never looked up to see if Mike had the ball [before he stepped out of bounds], which he didn't. So he dragged his feet, stepped out, and caught the ball. We laughed about it later. We got away with one there."

Penn State still had to make another play to win, still had 2 yards and nine seconds to go. The short-yardage offense came on the field again, with McCloskey lining up on the left side or strong side and Bowman on the right side or weak side.

Blackledge faked to Williams and looked for McCloskey in the left corner of the end zone, but he was covered. Bowman, never known for his quickness, gave the defensive end an outside fake, ran past the linebackers, and waved his arm in the back of the end zone. Blackledge's pass was low, but Bowman, the former defensive tackle and linebacker, caught it inches above the ground and was surrounded by teammates, cheerleaders, and fans.

"There was nobody else there," Bowman said. "As soon as I got past the linebacker, I was like, 'Hmmm.' After I caught it, I didn't realize the impact the play had. I did what I was supposed to do."

Wide receiver Kenny Jackson made forty-seven catches for 697 yards and seven touchdowns for Penn State in 1982.

"A lot of people on the Nebraska side thought Bowman didn't catch it," said Garrity, who watched from the sideline. "But he caught that ball. I know he caught that ball."

When Nebraska's kickoff return fell short, the crowd stormed the field, engulfed the players, and tore down the goalpost in the south end zone, depositing it on the steps of Old Main. The fans who stayed in the stands jumped up and down and celebrated for a long time, not wanting to leave.

"That's a Penn State crowd?" Bowman thought later when he watched the tape of the game. "They did a panoramic shot of the stadium and it was like a mountain of ants. It was nuts. It was one of the best crowds I've ever seen there. It was like a huge party.

"They're usually sitting down and cheering only when it's appropriate."

Two weeks later, the Lions lost 42–21 to Alabama on the road and thought their hopes for a national championship might be squashed. But they rebounded, beating Notre Dame and Pitt and receiving help from other teams. By the end of the regular season, they had moved to second in the rankings with a 10–1 record.

That set up a showdown against top-ranked Georgia in the Sugar Bowl in New Orleans, where Penn State turned back the undefeated Bulldogs 27–23 for their first national title.

"The Sugar Bowl and the win over Georgia were comparable," McCloskey said. "The Nebraska game was probably the most exciting game I played in. That game just seemed special because of where it was and how it happened. Maybe it's more special to me than to other people."

The game remains a painful memory to Nebraska players and fans. Blackledge and Radecic began their NFL careers with the Kansas City Chiefs, where they often came in contact with Nebraska fans who reminded them of Penn State's good fortune in 1982. "To this day, whenever I run into a Nebraska person, they still bring up that game," said Blackledge, who has worked as a network college football analyst since his retirement. "Of course, they still bring up that McCloskey was out of bounds. That was such a major issue."

Radecic played in the NFL for twelve seasons with Kansas City, Buffalo, and Indianapolis. "They'll make comments about us changing the dimensions of the field for that game," Radecic said. "Anybody who is a true fan of their school remembers those big games."

Garrity played in the NFL with the Pittsburgh Steelers and Philadelphia Eagles, where Nebraska's Dave Rimington was one of his teammates. But they never discussed the Penn State–Nebraska game.

Bowman has worked in sales and lives in a suburb of Fort Worth, Texas. Nebraska has been part of his sales region over the years, which means he has spent a lot of time in that state meeting a lot of people. He rarely has had to introduce himself.

"Nebraska people are so wonderful," Bowman said. "They are such great fans. Every single one of them has been more than cordial. Everyone in Nebraska knows who I am. I can almost guarantee you that. 'Oh, you're that guy.' "

One of Bowman's brothers-in-law bumped into Rimington in his travels. When he told Rimington who his brother-in-law was, Rimington immediately knew who Bowman was. "I have one of Dave Rimington's business cards," Bowman said. "On the back he signed it: 'Kirk: Go 'Huskers! Dave Rimington. P.S. You dropped the ball.' They had a good laugh over it."

McCloskey played four years in the NFL with the Houston Oilers and the Eagles. He still attends one or two

Penn State games a year with his family. He continues to run into people, whether they're from Nebraska or not, who remember his sideline catch.

"That happens a lot," he said. "An introduction is made and someone says, 'Yeah, I remember. You were the tight end who caught that pass out of bounds.' 'Well, that's me.' We just laugh.

"It didn't bother me that it was controversial. I was surprised by the vigor of some people. They thought that I, in some way, was dishonest, that I had some control over it. The referee made the call. All I did was catch the football."

The game remains one of the greatest wins in school history, ranking up with Penn State's win over Georgia in the Sugar Bowl for the 1982 national title and the Lions' win over top-ranked Miami in the Fiesta Bowl for the 1986 national crown.

"That day we realized we could play with the best and beat the best," Bowman said. "We could beat anybody. It was the culmination of the undefeated seasons in the '70s. A lot of people believe that was the game that put the program over the hump."

The Duel in the Desert

W hen they left the Orange Bowl on January 1, 1986, the Penn State Nittany Lions were disappointed but not crushed. They were angry, but they were not devastated.

The top-ranked Lions had just lost a chance at winning their second national title in three years, falling to number three Oklahoma 25–10. Their defense shut down the high-powered Sooners, except for two long plays that went for touchdowns, a 71-yard pass to tight end Keith Jackson and a 61-yard run by halfback Lydell Carr.

But eighteen starters were returning for Penn State and expecting to gain another crack at a national championship. "That loss obviously motivated us," said defensive end Bob White. "We knew how close we were to a goal that was very much attainable. When you get that close and taste it and don't get it, it takes things to another level for you."

With motivation and experience in tow in 1986, the Nittany Lions posted their second consecutive undefeated regular season. They gained the number two ranking and a spot in the Fiesta Bowl against top-ranked Miami, a highly anticipated matchup that NBC moved to January 2 for a prime-time telecast.

Pundits dubbed the game "The Duel in the Desert," between the guys in the white hats from Penn State and the guys in the black hats from Miami. Even though the Lions had won twenty-two of their last twenty-three games, few observers gave them a chance against the Hurricanes, who had Heisman Trophy winner Vinny Testaverde and several other future pros.

"We surprised all the people who did not give us respect or credit going into that game," White said. "No one believed we could pull that off. We knew each other. We knew what we were all about. 'Why are you guys even gonna show up? Those guys [Miami] are like a pro team.'

"That further motivated us. All those things plus our attitude helped us win that game."

"A lot of it had to do with the previous season," said quarterback John Shaffer. "We had tasted what the national championship game was like. We knew what it would be like. We had a number of us who had played.

"We knew we were going to win. That feeling permeated through the team. That confidence came from great coaching and great talent. It also was the function of being in close games and winning them."

Penn State began the 1986 season ranked sixth in the Associated Press poll and started 4–0 with wins over Temple, Boston College, East Carolina, and Rutgers. The Lions next faced 3–2 Cincinnati at Beaver Stadium and struggled to take a 14–7 halftime lead.

But the Bearcats rallied and Penn State trailed 17–14 when it got the ball at its 25 yard line with 5:57 to go. The Lions faced third and 10 and the possibility of their unbeaten season evaporating. But Shaffer found backup tailback Blair Thomas for a 32-yard gain to keep the drive alive. A few plays later, David Clark, another backup, scored from the 6 and

Shane Conlan later blocked a punt for safety to give Penn State a 23–17 victory.

"Whether the offense or defense was on the field, whether we were down three or seven points, we had an intangible, an inner confidence that we were going to win," Shaffer said. "We had some guys who really stepped up in unusual times, whether it was Dave Clark or someone else."

After routing longtime rival Syracuse 42–3, the sixth-ranked Lions traveled to Alabama to meet the second-ranked Crimson Tide, which was on a thirteen-game unbeaten streak and was favored by a touchdown. Alabama opened the scoring with a field goal and never crossed the Penn State 30 again.

The Lions' vaunted defense, led by linebackers Conlan, Pete Giftopoulos, Trey Bauer, and Don Graham, intercepted two passes, forced five fumbles, recovered three, and sacked quarterback Mike Shula five times in a 23–3 blowout. Bauer made nine tackles, Shaffer completed thirteen of seventeen passes without an interception, and Penn State jumped to number two in the polls.

"We had to go down there on their turf and show what we were made of," White said. "We pulled it off big time. It was another one of those confidence-builders. When you think about the route we took and the obstacles we overcame, for people who didn't want to give us credit was beyond me."

After a 19–0 shutout over West Virginia, another longtime rival, the Lions took on Maryland on a rainy afternoon at Beaver Stadium. D. J. Dozier helped set the tone by carrying twenty-five times for 111 yards and tackle Pete Curkendall returned an interception 82 yards to set up Dozier's touchdown that put Penn State ahead 14–3 with eight minutes left.

The Terrapins, behind quarterback Dan Henning, scored a quick touchdown but missed the two-point conversion. The

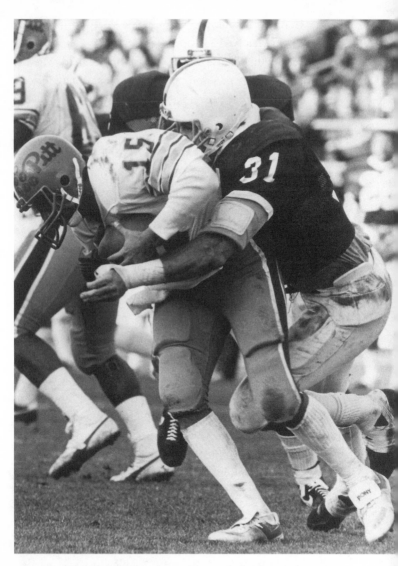

All-America linebacker Shane Conlan (31) intercepted two passes in Penn State's 14–10 win over Miami in the Fiesta Bowl, which enabled the Nittany Lions to win their second national title.

Lions drove for a field goal and a 17–9 lead with 1:04 to go, but Maryland and Henning were not finished.

Henning, who passed for 302 yards, found John Bonato for a 27-yard touchdown with seventeen seconds to go, cutting it to 17–15 and jeopardizing Penn State's perfect season. But on the two-point conversion, cornerback Duffy Cobbs broke up a pass for James Milling to enable the Lions to escape.

"You probably have to win one that maybe you don't deserve if you're going to go unbeaten," Penn State coach Joe Paterno said that day. "We've got to get the killer instinct and until we do we'll find ourselves in some tough games."

The Lions had another one the next week at South Bend, Indiana, where they took a 10–6 halftime lead over Notre Dame. Steve Beuerlein put the Irish ahead in the third quarter with a touchdown pass to Tim Brown, but Shaffer responded. He threw a touchdown pass to Ray Roundtree and ran for another score to make it 24–13.

"I remember that pass to Ray Roundtree," Shaffer said. "We had been setting up the defensive back on that side for two series. It was a play-action pass. Joe made the call. It was absolutely the perfect play. Ray was wide open. I told myself, 'Just don't mess this one up.'"

Notre Dame cut it to 24–19 early in the fourth quarter before Penn State punted. Beulerlein, who passed for 311 yards, led the Irish to a first down at the Penn State 6 in the closing moments, setting up one of the most memorable defensive stands in Lions' history.

On first down safety Ray Isom stopped Brown for a 3-yard loss on a run. On second down White sacked Beuerlein for a 9-yard loss back at the 18. On third down Gary Wilkerson broke up a pass in the end zone. After a short fourth-down pass went for 5 yards, the Lions ran out the clock.

"If I had to pick one game to remember in the regular season, it was Notre Dame," Shaffer said. "We knew it would be our toughest opponent and we were playing at Notre Dame."

"Notre Dame sticks out for me," White said. "That was a key, key moment for us."

After that game it was announced that number two Penn State would face number one Miami in the Fiesta Bowl as long as the Lions beat archrival Pittsburgh the next week. They took care of matters with an easy 34–14 win over the Panthers in a game that was marred by several fights.

"We're still that big, slow team with no talent wearing the black shoes, but playing for the national championship again," Bauer said after the Pitt game.

Penn State's meeting with Miami in the Fiesta Bowl in Tempe, Arizona, marked the first postseason game between undefeated teams in thirteen years. Adding to the drama, Sunkist kicked in enough money to become a title sponsor, increasing the payouts for each team and allowing NBC to move the game to prime time on January 2, 1987.

Few bowl games had received the attention and buildup that the Fiesta Bowl received. When the Hurricanes arrived in Arizona, several of them walked off the plane dressed in combat fatigues and said they were preparing for war. The next night at a bowl function that both teams attended, Miami All-America defensive tackle Jerome Brown led a walkout by the Hurricanes, asking, "Did the Japanese have dinner at Pearl Harbor before they bombed it?"

Defensive end Bob White, who felt that Penn State wasn't receiving proper respect, made a key sack to help preserve a 24–19 victory at Notre Dame late in the 1986 season.

The Penn State players took the pregame activities more calmly. They were accustomed to the surroundings and the attention after having played Oklahoma the year before. In that game Shaffer absorbed his first loss as a starting quarterback since he was in seventh grade. He threw three interceptions, lost a fumble, and blamed himself for the loss.

He was a favorite target for Nittany Lions fans who thought backup Matt Knizner should have been the starting quarterback. After the Orange Bowl, Paterno said he wasn't sure who would be the starter in 1986, even though Shaffer had been the regular for two seasons and had led Penn State to an 11–1 record.

A Pennsylvania newspaper conducted a fan poll in which Knizner trounced Shaffer.

"We came back in January and sat in Joe's office with Coach Bob [Phillips, the quarterbacks coach]," Shaffer said. "Joe said, 'We'll figure out who the starting quarterback will be before the first game.'

"From that meeting on it was a competition. We talked and we were friends, but we were competitive. It was the most important thing in our lives. I felt it was embarrassing that I had to re-earn the position. I can't describe it, but I never felt more pressure than I did then."

Shaffer won the job and found out two nights before the opener against Temple. He didn't have a great season statistically, completing 55.9 percent of his passes for just nine touchdowns. But he threw just four interceptions and made several clutch plays.

A few nights before the Fiesta Bowl, Shaffer, tight end Brian Siverling, and offensive linemen Dan Morgan and Mark Sickler went out to eat. As Shaffer was getting out of the backseat of the car, Morgan slammed the door and locked it on

Special Delivery

John Shaffer unwittingly began a ritual during his sophomore year at Penn State that he continued until he played his final game. One Friday afternoon in the fall, Shaffer and a couple friends decided they were hungry for stromboli and went to Brothers Pizza, then and now a popular haunt for students on College Avenue in State College.

"I noticed that every time I had it, we won the next day," Shaffer said.

He became the Nittany Lions' starting quarterback late in the 1984 season and made sure that he went to Brothers every Friday the following season. Penn State won all 11 games in the 1985 regular season before they traveled to Florida, where they lost to Oklahoma in the Orange Bowl for the national title.

It was the only game that Shaffer lost as a starting quarterback and the last time he failed to eat a Brothers stromboli before a game.

With Shaffer at quarterback, the Lions went 11-0 again in the regular season in 1986 and faced Miami in the Fiesta Bowl for the national title. He didn't want to end the streak, so he had stromboli from Brothers flown out to Arizona, site of the game.

"I can still remember sitting at the table having stromboli at the pregame meal," Shaffer said. "I know it was there two days before the game and it was frozen. It was terrible. I didn't care. I had to eat it."

Shaffer kept his stromboli streak alive, and so did Penn State. They beat the Hurricanes 14-10 and won their second national championship.

Shaffer's left hand. When the door was opened, Shaffer fell back into the car and passed out for about ten minutes.

"The skin was cut and swollen," Shaffer said. "For half a practice I had trouble taking snaps. I was very, very lucky. It's comical now."

Shaffer was ready for the game and so was the Penn State defense. Miami had averaged more than thirty-eight points per game during the regular season with Testaverde, powerful running backs Alonzo Highsmith and Melvin Bratton, and a fleet group of receivers led by Michael Irvin. Defensive coordinator Jerry Sandusky devised a scheme in which the Lions would rush just three players and disguise their pass coverages. "We wanted to create confusion and flood the passing lanes," White said. "Jerry just felt it was better to use three down linemen instead of four. It worked."

The Hurricanes arrived at Sun Devil Stadium in combat fatigues and taunted the Lions during pregame warm-ups. But when the game began, underdog Penn State showed it belonged.

Miami opened the scoring in the second quarter after Brown sacked Shaffer and forced a fumble deep in Penn State territory. Four plays later, Bratton scored from the 1 to make it 7–0. The Lions, though, responded with their only scoring drive.

Shaffer directed Penn State on a 74-yard march, hitting Eric Hamilton on a 24-yard pass. Tim Manoa ran for 19 yards and caught a 12-yard pass to set up Shaffer's 4-yard rollout that tied it 7–7 at the half.

"Joe was able to get everything out of that team that we had to give," Shaffer said. "We were not in the same category as Miami in terms of the number of athletes. We knew how to win. We were unselfish."

In the third quarter Conlan, playing with a sore knee and ankle, intercepted Testaverde to stop one threat. Shaffer also threw an interception, and both teams missed field goals, keeping it at 7–7 going into the fourth.

Mark Seelig kicked a 38-yard field goal to put Miami ahead early in the fourth quarter before the Hurricanes got the ball back after stopping the Lions. But Conlan stepped in front of a Testaverde pass at the Miami 44 and limped to the 5 before being tackled.

Shaffer fumbled the snap on first down, losing a yard. On second down Dozier took a pitch and scored with 8:13 to go for a 14–10 lead, which was not safe.

The Penn State defense forced a fumble and held the Hurricanes on downs. But Miami got one more shot in the closing moments. Starting from his 23 yard line with 3:07 to go, Testaverde led his team down the field, converting a 31-yard completion to Bennie Blades on fourth down.

"Every snap was a fight for your life," White said. "We didn't want to leave anything out there. We wanted to get after them. We had to figure out a way to make something happen."

With eighteen seconds remaining, the Hurricanes had a fourth and goal from the Penn State 13. Testaverde looked for Brett Perriman in the left corner of the end zone. But Giftopoulos dropped deep and made his second interception of the game, falling on the ball on the 10 yard line with nine seconds to go.

"I was standing on the 44 yard line, which is my lucky number," Shaffer said. "'Holy cow, this can't come down to him making a pass and it's over.' I forget who I was standing next to. I felt a lot more comfortable things were gonna work out when I saw where I was standing."

Shaffer jogged onto the field to take the final snap before a half-hour celebration ensued on the field. Penn State capped its one-hundredth season of football by winning its second national championship in five seasons, despite running fifty-nine plays to Miami's ninety-three. Conlan was named the outstanding defensive player of the game after making eight tackles and two interceptions, and Dozier was named the outstanding offensive player after rushing for 99 yards.

"I can't put into words how happy I am for these kids," Paterno said then. "They worked hard, believed in themselves, and had the poise to withstand pressure."

The game remains the most-watched college football game of all time with more than seventy million viewers.

"What we had was something very hard to create or find," White said. "We truly had a group of guys who thoroughly enjoyed playing the game and each other. We cared about each other. We enjoyed each other and fought for one another.

"There was a genuine love and concern for one another and that translated into all those wonderful things. They're all the things that define a team."

Tailback D. J. Dozier, the only player to lead the Nittany Lions in rushing four times (1983–86), scored the game-winning touchdown against Miami in the Fiesta Bowl.

Unbeaten and Uncrowned–Again

L ess than a half hour earlier, Penn State had completed a decisive victory in the Rose Bowl and a 12–0 season. They floated off the field and into the locker room, waving their index fingers and wearing wide smiles. They became the first Big Ten team to go unbeaten and untied since 1968. They averaged 512.7 total yards per game, a conference record, and forty-seven points, the most by a Big Ten team since 1916.

Yet the 1994 Nittany Lions had conflicting emotions because they knew they were going to remain number two in the polls behind Nebraska. They knew they were not going to win the national championship.

"In some ways, it's very frustrating," Penn State coach Joe Paterno said. "But God didn't mean everything to be fair in life. It's frustrating to realize we should have six or seven national championships."

It was the fourth time that one of Paterno's teams at Penn State had finished unbeaten, untied, and uncrowned. The three previous times (1968, 1969, 1973), the Nittany Lions had been criticized for playing a soft schedule. But this time, they were the champions of the mighty Big Ten with victories over Michigan, Ohio State, and Southern Cal.

They actually had dropped from number one to number two in one poll after a 63–14 blowout of twenty-first ranked Ohio State and then in the other poll after a 35–29 win over Indiana, a game in which the Hoosiers scored two touchdowns in the final two minutes. No wonder they were so confused and so defiant.

"It's not difficult to accept," cornerback Brian Miller said, "because I've already accepted it. I'm not even going to look at the polls. All they have to do is bring on Nebraska."

"We're going to crown ourselves national champions, how does that sound?" quarterback Kerry Collins said. "We're going to have a ring with a lot of diamonds and big, fat '1' in the middle of it."

Winning the national championship might have been on the minds of the Lions when preseason practice began in August, but they also had concerns. Three of their best players—tailback Ki-Jana Carter, tight end Kyle Brady, and linebacker Brian Gelzheiser—missed spring practice with injuries. Then defensive tackle Eric Clair suffered a knee injury that knocked him out of the first four games.

Paterno worried about the defense, which returned just three starters and would sustain several injuries during the season, as early as the spring. "If we're to be competitive in the Big Ten, it'll still depend on how good we are on defense," he said.

Seven starters returned on offense, which had scored more than thirty-two points a game the year before: Collins, Carter, Brady, fullbacks Brian Milne and Jon Witman, and receivers Bobby Engram and Freddie Scott. Jeff Hartings and Marco Rivera were the only returning starters on the offensive line, but Bucky Greeley, Andre Johnson, and Keith Conlin

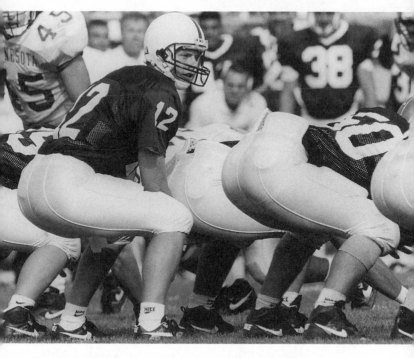

Kerry Collins won the Maxwell Award as the nation's top player and the Davey O'Brien Award as the nation's top quarterback in 1994 and directed an offense that gained 512.7 yards per game.

had seen playing time. Confidence was in the air as Penn State began the season ranked ninth in both major polls.

"Everybody thinks we're going to go out and score fifty points a game, like it's easy," Collins said.

The Lions made it look easy in their opener at Minnesota, where they crushed the Golden Gophers 56–3 and gained 689 total yards, just 22 off the school record. Collins completed nineteen of twenty-three passes for 260 yards and three touchdowns, including a school-record fourteen straight completions. Carter carried twenty times for 210 yards and three touchdowns.

Penn State showed almost perfect balance, gaining 345 yards on the ground and 344 through the air. The first-team offense left the game in the middle of the third quarter, a harbinger of the rest of the season. "They tried to stop our run, so we got them with the pass," Carter said. "If we keep trying to get better, it's going to be pretty hard to stop our offense. We do have a lot of weapons."

"Don't get too carried away with this one," Paterno said. "We have a long way to go yet."

Penn State stepped up in class the next week when USC came to Beaver Stadium. The Trojans had opened the season with an easy win over Washington and had moved up to number fourteen in one poll. They also had highly regarded Rob Johnson at quarterback, but it was not a contest.

The Lions scored in the first 1:15 when Carter ran 32 yards and scored two more times in the first eight minutes for a 21–0 lead. They led the stunned Trojans 35–0 at the half and coasted to a 38–14 victory. Collins passed for 248 yards and two touchdowns, Carter ran for 119 yards and one touchdown, and Scott caught six passes for 133 yards as Penn State gained 534 yards.

"I think they overwhelmed us," USC coach John Robinson said, "got us on our heels and could do whatever they wanted to us. They look as good a football team as I've seen."

The voters in the polls were only slightly impressed, ranking Penn State sixth as it prepared to take on Iowa at home. The Hawkeyes were 2–0 with eight returning starters on offense, but they were overmatched, too.

The Lions rolled up a 42–0 lead in the first sixteen minutes on their way to a 61–21 demolition, the most points allowed by a Hayden Fry team at Iowa. Carter carried eleven times for 89 yards and two touchdowns, while Collins completed five of seven passes for 98 yards in limited action. With Penn State attempting just thirteen passes, eleven backs rushed for 309 yards. "I was afraid something like this would happen," Fry said. "I told Coach Paterno I voted them number one in the coaches' poll and they didn't do anything to change my mind."

"Shoot, they could win the national championship," Iowa quarterback Ryan Driscoll said. "The Penn State offense is untouchable. They have no reason to lose."

Paterno, of course, remained guarded, refusing to go beyond saying that the Lions had a lot of potential. "We haven't been in a situation where we're down and groping for something to do," he said. "It's not happening. What are we going to do from our own 5 yard line with six minutes to go and we need a drive?"

Paterno and Penn State would find out later in the season. Over the next five games, the Lions faced their first challenges and their banged-up defense would come under fire.

The Lions, who moved up to fifth in the polls, hammered Rutgers 55–27 as Collins went fourteen for sixteen for 328 yards and two touchdowns. But the Scarlet Knights moved the football with ease, gaining 513 total yards, and were within 27–20 late in the first half. Penn State scored with five seconds to go in the half to go up 34–20 and broke it open in the second half, but the defense struggled.

Collins, on the other hand, was exceptional, posting what was then the third-highest passing total in school history. He overthrew Engram on his first attempt and Engram dropped a sure touchdown pass, but they were the only incompletions. Collins hit Scott on an 82-yard strike for one touchdown and Engram caught eight passes for 200 yards.

Collins was scheduled to be the starter as a sophomore in 1992, but he broke his right index finger right before preseason camp opened. He shared time with John Sacca until the third game of the 1993 season, when Collins took over for good. "I think Kerry is playing as well as any quarterback who's ever played for us," Paterno said. "As long as he stays as hot as he is, we'll be a very good offensive team."

Ranked fourth, Penn State faced even more adversity the next week in Philadelphia against Temple. Carter suffered a dislocated thumb late in the first half after gaining 178 all-purpose yards and watched the second half from the sideline. The Lions trailed after the first quarter for the first time all season before going on to win 48–21.

Collins passed for 286 yards and three touchdowns, and Engram and Scott both topped 100 receiving yards. Penn State gained 596 total yards, 10.6 per play, but Paterno was steamed over the defense's play.

"If we play that way the rest of the season, we might lose three or four games," he said.

Fortunately for Carter and the Lions, they had a bye the next Saturday and had two weeks to prepare for Michigan, something Wolverines coach Gary Moeller brought up often. Penn State was ranked third and Michigan, which had lost to Colorado on a Hail Mary pass, was fifth.

Carter, who played with a splint on his thumb, rushed for 165 yards on twenty-six carries and helped the Lions take a 16–0 lead in the second quarter. But the Wolverines rebounded, wiping out the deficit to take a 17–16 lead in the third quarter on Tyrone Wheatley's second touchdown run to the delight of the Michigan Stadium crowd.

Collins, who passed for 231 yards and three touchdowns, was brilliant in the second half. He put the Lions ahead 24–17

Tailback Ki-Jana Carter suffered a dislocated thumb in the middle of the 1994 season before going on to rush for 1,539 yards and twenty-three touchdowns.

with a 9-yard pass to Witman and a conversion pass to Scott. The Wolverines tied it one more time early in the fourth quarter before Penn State delivered.

Carter ran 26 yards on a draw play and Collins found Engram in the back of the end zone for a 16-yard score with 2:53 left. Miller's last-minute interception sealed the Lions' biggest win since beating Miami for the 1986 national championship.

"I didn't think they'd do that to our defense," Moeller said.

It was Penn State's first win over a team ranked in the top five in four years and it propelled the Lions to the number one spot in both polls. "We've played well enough to be considered number one," Collins said. "We have as much right as anybody to be number one. . . . They say that the road to the Rose Bowl goes through Ann Arbor. This was a big step for us."

Two weeks later, during which Penn State had another bye, number twenty-one Ohio State came to Happy Valley with a 6–2 record and as the last team to beat the Lions. The Buckeyes kept it close in the first quarter and trailed 7–0 before their world collapsed.

Penn State scored four touchdowns in the second quarter to take a stunning 35–0 halftime lead. The Lions had perfect balance on offense, running for 286 yards and passing for 286, as they pulverized the Buckeyes 63–14 and handed them their worst loss since 1946. It was the most points allowed by Ohio State since 1902.

Collins completed nineteen of twenty-three passes for 265 yards and two touchdowns; Carter carried nineteen times for 137 yards and four touchdowns; Engram caught six passes for 102 yards and a TD. The defense played one of its finest games of the year, holding Ohio State to 214 total yards and intercepting three passes.

"We just had one of those days," Paterno said. "We did everything right."

"I thought we made a statement," Collins said. "We beat a good team and we beat them resoundingly. I'd be miffed if we weren't still number one."

Collins and his teammates were miffed. The Lions beat a team that wound up finishing second in the Big Ten and 9–4 for the season by forty-nine points, yet they dropped to number two in the Associated Press poll. Third-ranked Nebraska had beaten second-ranked Colorado the same day and took over the number one spot by six points. In the coaches' poll Penn State held on to the top spot by two points.

Penn State dropped to number two in both polls the next week after a sloppy performance in a 35–29 win over Indiana, a game in which the Hoosiers scored fifteen points in the final two minutes. The Lions were never in danger of losing the game and had two touchdowns wiped out by penalties in the fourth quarter, but that didn't matter when the polls were released.

Nebraska held an eighteen-point lead in the AP poll and a twenty-seven-point lead in the coaches' poll.

"I don't care about the polls," Paterno snapped after the Indiana game. "What do I care about the polls?"

The polls were the furthest thing from the minds of the Lions a week later at Illinois, where they fell behind 21–0 after the first quarter. They cut it to 28–14 at the half and 31–21 going into the fourth quarter. Penn State converted a fourth and 2 from the Illinois 41 and scored on Milne's short run.

Penn State's weary defense held, but Illinois punter Brett Larsen booted a 67-yard kick, pinning the Lions back at their 4 yard line trailing 31–28 with 6:07 left. It was exactly the test Paterno said two months earlier that Penn State needed to pass before he anointed them a great team.

"Ninety-six yards, fellas," Collins said as he trotted into the huddle with the rain and the wind in his face. "Let's go. Let's do it."

The Lions used fourteen plays, converted three third downs and watched Collins go seven for seven. Milne capped it with a 2-yard burst with fifty-seven seconds to go, his fourth touchdown. Kim Herring intercepted Johnny Johnson's desperation pass in the end zone as time ran out, clinching

Penn State's first Big Ten title and their first trip to the Rose Bowl since 1923.

"That was a great comeback," Paterno said, "because Illinois played so well. Our kids hung in there and Kerry made some great passes. That was a super drive."

That day, Nebraska struggled to beat Iowa State 28–12, a team which had lost to Iowa 37–9 early in the season. But Penn State didn't gain ground on the Cornhuskers and seemed headed for a second place finish if both teams finished unbeaten.

The Lions routed Northwestern 45–17 and Michigan State 59–31 to go 11–0 and give Paterno his seventh undefeated regular season. The win over Northwestern was strange; Penn State led 38–3 at the half and had the ball less than six minutes. Against Michigan State, Carter and Collins made their final pitches for the Heisman Trophy.

In what turned out to be his final game at Beaver Stadium, Carter carried twenty-seven times for 227 yards and five touchdowns to push his junior year total to 1,539, just 28 off Lydell Mitchell's school record. Collins completed sixteen of twenty-four passes for 289 yards and one touchdown, giving him a 2,679 yards, 176 completions, a 66.7 completion percentage, and a 172.9 efficiency rating, all school records.

"They're as explosive an offensive team as I've seen in a decade," Michigan State coach George Perles said. "They lived up to their reputation."

Engram capped his junior year with eight catches for 169 yards and one touchdown against Michigan State, giving him a school-record 1,029 yards for the year. He became the inaugural winner of the Biletnikoff Award, presented to the nation's top receiver.

Engram was one of five Penn State offensive players to receive All-America first-team honors, along with Carter,

Wide receiver Bobby Engram caught fifty-two passes for 1,029 yards and seven touchdowns in 1994 and was selected the inaugural winner of the Biletnikoff Award, presented to the nation's top receiver.

Collins, Brady, and Hartings. Collins also was named the winner of the Maxwell Award, presented to the nation's outstanding player; the Davey O'Brien Award, presented to the nation's top quarterback; and the Big Ten MVP award.

Two days later at the Heisman Trophy presentation, it was clear that Carter and Collins canceled each other out in the voting. Colorado running back Rashaan Salaam easily won the Heisman, followed by Carter in second and Collins in fourth. Carter and Collins were slightly disappointed.

"I'm happy as long as my teammates respect me," Collins said. "That's the most gratifying thing. These personal awards, I get embarrassed."

Once the awards were handed out, the Lions focused their attention on the Rose Bowl and Pac-10 champion Oregon. Because Penn State was tied to the Rose Bowl as the Big Ten champion and because Nebraska was tied to the Orange Bowl as the Big Eight champion, the teams were unable to meet in a bowl game to settle the national championship.

Nebraska played third-ranked Miami in the Orange Bowl on New Year's night before the Lions faced 9–3 Oregon in the Rose Bowl on January 2. The Cornhuskers turned back the Hurricanes 24–17, all but locking up coach Tom Osborne's first national championship.

Penn State could have beaten Oregon by fifty points and it wouldn't have mattered. With Danny O'Neil passing for a Rose Bowl–record 456 yards, the Ducks stayed close until the Lions broke a tie in the middle of the third quarter with two quick scores. The Lions went on to win 38–20 as Carter ran for

156 yards and three touchdowns and Collins passed for 200 yards.

"Penn State has my vote," Oregon coach Rich Brooks said. "I voted for them in the coaches' poll going into the game and I have no reason to feel differently. They are the best offensive machine I have seen."

"I don't think there's anybody out there who could stop us," Carter said. "It may be one of the greatest offenses ever, definitely at Penn State."

Nebraska (13–0) finished number one in both polls, receiving fifty-four first-place votes in the coaches' poll and fifty-one and a half in the AP poll. Penn State (12–0) received eight first-place votes in the coaches' poll and ten and a half in the AP poll.

Some voters said later they voted for the Cornhuskers because Osborne had never won a national championship and Paterno had won two. "Even though they [the voters] feel sorry for Tom Osborne," Carter said, "I haven't got a national championship and neither have my teammates."

Penn State beat five bowl teams by an average of 20.2 points and won the title in a conference that was number one in computer rankings. The Lions also played what the NCAA rated the seventeenth-toughest schedule in the country; Nebraska's schedule was rated the fifty-seventh toughest.

"It is a shame that the two best teams in the country didn't even face each other," Collins said. "Until that happens, if you have two unbeaten teams after the season, I don't think you can crown one of them national champion.

"I'm not going to let them take away from what I've experienced. We're going to name ourselves national champions, regardless of what all the people who sit in their La-Z-Boys on Saturdays and what all the coaches say."

Penn State's snub played a huge role in the major conferences forming the Bowl Championship Series, which pits the top two teams in the country in a bowl game. That fact hardly remains a consolation to the Nittany Lions.

"That was as good a football team as I've ever been around," Paterno said. "I don't know of any team I've had that could beat them. I don't know of any team in the country that could beat them."

Larry Johnson's Season to Remember

One of his coaches said that Larry Johnson did not discriminate in practice; he unloaded on the biggest lineman or the smallest manager.

His father said he often encouraged him to loosen up. His brother said trying to talk to him was like "trying to talk to a brick wall." His quarterback said he "runs like he's ticked off."

Larry Johnson carried a chip on his shoulder the size of Idaho in 2002 to the greatest season by a running back in Penn State history and one of the greatest seasons in the history of the sport. He rushed for 2,087 yards and twenty touchdowns, led the nation in rushing and all-purpose yards, and won the Maxwell Award and the Walter Camp Player of the Year Award as the nation's outstanding player.

"I'm not a person who likes to stay relaxed," Johnson said. "If you stay too relaxed, you kind of forget about things and things get out of focus."

Johnson's career at Penn State was clouded in 2000 when he vented his frustration after the Nittany Lions' shocking 24–6 loss to Toledo at Beaver Stadium. In that game they gained just 166 total yards and Johnson carried three times for 7 yards and caught a 61-yard pass for Penn State's only score.

A sophomore then, Johnson allowed his impatience to get the best of him when he took aim at the Penn State coaching staff, which included his father, Larry Sr., the defensive line coach. "It's the system," he said. "We have coaches who have been here twenty, thirty years. It seems like things never change. We run the same offense. Teams that play us know where we're going to run. Everything we do is too predictable. Everybody knows what we're doing."

Johnson refrained from saying anything else outrageous until the end of his career. For the rest of the 2000 season and 2001, he continued to share time with as many as three other teammates. The tailback-by-committee system failed miserably and so did the Penn State running game in those two seasons.

The Nittany Lions ran the football poorly mostly because opponents stacked the line with seven and eight men. They made a slight improvement when a spread offense and freshman quarterback Zack Mills were installed in the middle of the 2001 season. But the school that produced John Cappelletti, Franco Harris, Curt Warner, D. J. Dozier, Blair Thomas, Ki-Jana Carter, and Curtis Enis rushed for a meager 1,317 yards, the worst total in school history.

Johnson rushed for 337 yards, the lowest total by a Penn State season leader since quarterback Richie Lucas ran for 325 in 1959. Yet Johnson always seemed to be in a hurry when he carried the ball. A powerful back (6'2", 222) with deceptive speed, he didn't pick his holes well. He often seemed bent on making a big play and running through defenders instead of around them.

But when 2002 arrived, Johnson was clearly the number one tailback and looked forward to receiving the opportunity to show off his skills. Few people outside Pennsylvania had heard of him, even though he led the Big Ten in kickoff returning in 2001. He was rarely mentioned among the nation's top running backs when the season began.

"It's been a long time coming, but it's here," Johnson said. "It'll feel good because then I won't have to rush myself or feel like I have to get 60 yards when I go in there or break a long one. I can take my time and be patient."

Johnson got off to a strong start against Central Florida, carrying eighteen times for 92 yards, catching four passes for 30 yards and one touchdown, and returning a kickoff 53 yards for 175 all-purpose yards.

He then put together back-to-back 100-yard games, picking up 123 yards against Nebraska and 147 against Louisiana Tech, as Penn State opened 3–0. Johnson seemed to be at peace with himself on and off the field.

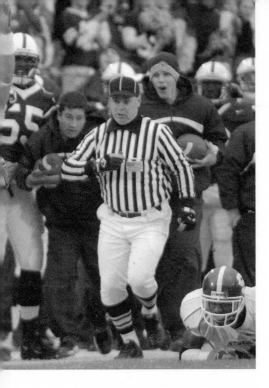

Larry Johnson runs for a 38-yard touchdown against Michigan State in November 2002 and becomes the ninth back in Division I-A history to rush for 2,000 yards in a regular season. (Steve Manuel)

"He's relaxed a little bit, knowing he's the guy," Mills said. "He still runs with a passion. He almost seems really angry. At times he seemed like that off the field."

A few nights after a 49–17 win over Louisiana Tech, Johnson took the starting offensive linemen, two fullbacks, and tight ends to a State College restaurant, where he picked up the tab for ribs and chicken wings. It was a surprising turn of events. Two years earlier, during his outburst after the Toledo loss, he blasted the offensive linemen.

"I just wanted them to know that I appreciate what they're doing," Johnson said. "They only get noticed when they miss a block or something. I'm going to need them more than they're going to need me."

Johnson had a terrific game the next week in a wild 42–35 overtime loss to Iowa at Beaver Stadium. Although the Hawkeyes' second-ranked run defense held him to 68 rushing yards, Johnson scored two touchdowns, caught six passes for 93 yards, and returned five kickoffs for 72 yards. He gained 233 all-purpose yards, but strangely his performance was held against him later in the season.

At unbeaten Wisconsin, Johnson rushed for 111 yards, gained 171 all-purpose yards and scored on a 24-yard run that gave Penn State the lead for good in a 34–31 victory. But he left the game early in the third quarter with a hamstring injury that kept him out of the starting lineup the next week at Michigan.

Backup quarterback Michael Robinson started at tailback at Ann Arbor, but Johnson quickly entered the game and scored the Nittany Lions' first touchdown on a 17-yard draw play. He went on to rush for 78 yards on seventeen carries and caught five passes for 46 yards in a game Penn State led four times. Michigan won 27–24 in overtime after Mills's pass to Tony Johnson, Larry's brother, was ruled incomplete inside the Wolverines' 25 in the final minute of regulation.

Penn State coach Joe Paterno kept the players off-limits from the media after the game and made some terse remarks. A few days later, Paterno questioned the integrity of the Big Ten officials who worked the game. Athletic Director Tim Curley asked the conference to undertake a comprehensive review of its officiating.

Larry Johnson was having a very nice season, but few people noticed. That was about to change.

On Homecoming weekend at Penn State, Johnson gave the returning alumni something to remember. He carried twenty-three times for a school-record 257 yards and two touchdowns in a 49–0 blowout of Northwestern. He made five runs of more than 20 yards and broke Curt Warner's record of 256 yards set in 1981 at Syracuse. He left the game after his second score with 13:18 left in the third quarter. "It means a lot," Johnson said of the record. "This is dedicated to guys like Curt Warner, D. J. Dozier, Curtis Enis, and Ki-Jana Carter who have always encouraged me in my career."

A month earlier, Warner had made his first trip to Penn State in nearly twenty years to attend the reunion of the Nittany Lions' 1982 national championship team. He talked to the 2002 Lions and reminded them of the importance of the team concept. A preseason Heisman Trophy contender in 1982, Warner sulked when the spotlight shifted to quarterback Todd Blackledge, who threw four touchdown passes in each of the first three games.

But in the end, Blackledge's emergence created balance on offense and helped Penn State win its first national title.

"Curt kind of put everything into perspective for me," Johnson said. "He wanted the ball more and he had to step back, too, for the team. It was the best thing not to think about himself all the time."

Johnson helped Penn State trample past Northwestern for 423 rushing yards, its highest total in sixteen years. On one of his runs near the end of the first half, he ran over his brother, who was blocking downfield. He followed Tony's two down-field blocks for a 60-yard run early in the third quarter before he left the game.

"He's a very aggressive kid, very competitive," Paterno said. "I don't have any problem with Larry. He works like a dog in practice. He's a little moody sometimes, but so is my wife."

Johnson actually was laughing on the sidelines, a departure for the angry young man. Afterward, he wore a steel-blue

Muhammad Ali warm-up suit and cracked a smile when someone suggested that he did not float like a butterfly, like Ali.

"Yeah," he said, "but I try to sting like a bee."

The Nittany Lions traveled to Ohio Stadium, a hornet's nest for them since joining the Big Ten. They had not reached double figures in their four previous conference games at Ohio State and had absorbed a 45–6 shellacking in 2000, the worst loss in Paterno's career.

Johnson opened the scoring with a 5-yard run in the first quarter, one of only four rushing touchdowns allowed by the Buckeyes in the regular season. He set it up with a 35-yard run, but he and the Penn State offense struggled the rest of the dreary afternoon. The Lions gained 179 total yards and Johnson had a season-low 66 rushing yards, an outing that was brought up often late in the season.

Ohio State pulled out a 13–7 victory on Chris Gamble's 40-yard interception return in the third quarter. The Buckeyes went on to win the Big Ten title and the national championship with a 14–0 record, but that was of little consolation to the Nittany Lions or Johnson. "I think that's the best I've seen our defense play since I've been here," Johnson said. "For us to come up with nothing on offense is ridiculous. I felt we owed them more than what we were doing for them. We didn't hold up our end of the deal."

They did against Illinois the next week at Beaver Stadium. Johnson broke the school record for rushing yards in a game for the second time in three weeks, carrying a career-high thirty-one times for 279 yards and one touchdown in an 18–7 win. He also became the ninth back in Penn State history to run for 1,000 yards in a season and the first since Enis in 1997.

Johnson, however, seemed more concerned with his fumble on the 10-yard carry that broke the record in the third quarter. "I'm more angry that I fumbled on that play," Johnson said. "That made me more disappointed."

He made a spectacular 84-yard run in the first quarter, sidestepping two Illinois defenders near the line of scrimmage and outracing two others to the end zone. It was the longest run by a Penn State back in sixteen years. Johnson almost matched it in the fourth quarter, but a holding penalty wiped out another 84-yard run.

"I'm just excited when I watch him on the Jumbotron," Penn State defensive end Michael Haynes said. "I'm just excited. I'm like, 'Run! Run!' He's such a powerful runner. It's really hard to tackle him."

Virginia also had trouble bringing down Johnson, who ran thirty-one times for 188 yards in a one-sided 35–14 victory. He gained 251 all-purpose yards, which gave him a school-record 1,959 yards for the season and moved him into first in the nation. He widened his Big Ten rushing lead and moved to third in the nation in rushing.

He started to appear on Heisman Trophy watch lists across the country and began to merit national attention. Earlier that week, ESPN's Mel Kiper Jr. projected that Johnson would be a fourth- or fifth-round pick in the NFL draft in April 2003. "I'm surprised," Johnson said. "That fuels me to go out there and do the best I can. I like to hear guys put me down and say I can't do this or I can't do that."

He could do no wrong the following week at Indiana. On a field that looked like and felt like a beach on the New Jersey shore, Johnson had a ball. He carried twenty-eight times for 327 yards and four touchdowns in a 58–25 rout of the Hoosiers. He set a school record for the third time in five games, set a Memorial Stadium record, and posted the fifth-highest rushing total in Big Ten history.

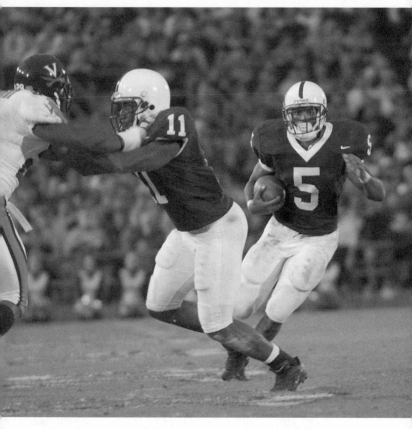

Larry Johnson follows a block by his brother Tony, a wide receiver, to make a long gain against Virginia in November 2002. (Steve Manuel)

Johnson also smashed Lydell Mitchell's thirty-one-year-old school record for yards in a season (1,567 in 1971) and moved to 1,736 for the season. He scored on runs of 69, 43, 1, and 41 yards and continued his late surge in the Heisman campaign.

"I can't tell you whether he's the best player in the country," Paterno said. "But if they consider a running back, they have to consider Larry Johnson. The numbers are there and he's coming on strong. He deserves a lot of consideration. He's as explosive as any player I've seen this year."

He'd averaged 11.7 yards per carry against the Hoosiers and outgained the Indiana offense by himself. "I'd say he's got to be one of the better halfbacks that I've ever seen," Indiana coach Gerry DiNardo said. "He's in a very elite group. He has a little bit of his own style. He's a big back who has better speed than most good backs his size. I think that's what separates him from the rest."

Johnson saved his best for his last home game. The tears and the yards flowed at Beaver Stadium, where he ran for 279 yards and four touchdowns—all in the first half—as Penn State poleaxed hapless Michigan State 61–7 on Senior Day.

He became the ninth back in Division I-A history and the first in Big Ten history to rush for 2,000 yards in a regular season. He reached the milestone with a 38-yard touchdown run on his final carry with 2:33 left in the first half.

Johnson fought back tears before the game and fought off the Spartans during the game, carrying just nineteen times and averaging a mind-boggling 14.7 yards per carry. He finished the regular season with 2,015 yards and averaged 167.9 yards per game.

"He's like a man playing against boys out there," Paterno said.

On second and 8 from the Michigan State 38 late in the second quarter, offensive coordinator Fran Ganter called "48 Sweep" with the crowd rising in anticipation. Needing 23 yards for 2,000, Johnson found a crease between left tackle Gus Felder and left guard Chris McKelvy and broke through it into history.

"Before the season we wanted to get him over 1,000 yards," offensive tackle Matt Schmitt said. "Over 2,000 was something we couldn't even comprehend. We feel pretty damn good."

It was a stunning turn of events for someone who spent his first three seasons at Penn State sharing time in the backfield and who briefly considered transferring after making his caustic remarks about the coaching staff in 2000.

"All he needed was a chance," Tony Johnson said. "He's cashing in on his chance."

Larry Johnson spent the next few weeks watching and listening to the Heisman Trophy debate. He emerged as one of the five leading candidates with Iowa quarterback Brad Banks, Miami quarterback Ken Dorsey, Miami running back Willis McGahee, and USC quarterback Carson Palmer.

Johnson's critics were quick to point out that he did not rush for 100 yards in Penn State's three losses—to Iowa, Michigan, and Ohio State. They ignored his all-purpose yardage and that he scored in each of those games. He lashed out at them three days before the Heisman Trophy winner was announced.

"A lot of people said I should be enjoying it and it's a once-in-a-lifetime experience," Johnson said on the day he was invited to New York for the Heisman ceremony. "But I'm still in a fighting mood. I still hear more bad than good. There are so many people who run their mouths who really don't know what it takes to have a season like that. I concentrate on those people more than I do my success."

The next night, though, in Orlando, Florida, Johnson made off with some impressive hardware at the College Football Awards Show. He received the Maxwell Award, the Walter Camp Player of the Year Award as the nation's outstanding player, and the Doak Walker Award as the nation's outstanding running back.

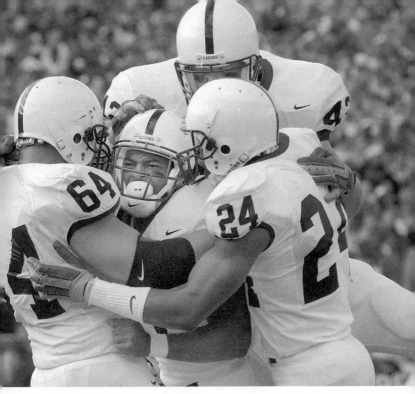

Larry Johnson won the Maxwell Award, the Walter Camp Award, and the Doak Walker Award, and he finished third in voting for the Heisman Trophy. (Steve Manuel)

"Deep down, I kind of thought I deserved the Walker Award," Johnson said. "But the Maxwell and the Walter Camp were a total surprise."

The previous three players who won the Maxwell, Camp, and Walker Awards in the same year—Ron Dayne (1999), Ricky Williams (1998), and Eddie George (1995)—went on to win the Heisman. But Johnson did not. He finished third behind Palmer, the winner, and Banks, the runner-up. Yet Johnson handled the evening with class and appeared to be more relaxed and relieved than at any other time in his Penn State career. He smiled for the photographers and cracked jokes.

"I got more than I expected out of this deal," Johnson said. "All my trophies pretty much add up to the Heisman Trophy. I'm still going home with three trophies. I got my fair share. You can't be greedy."

Larry Johnson, however, wasn't content after the final game of his career, Penn State's 13–9 loss to Auburn in the Capital One Bowl in Orlando. He carried twenty times for 72 yards, slipped a few times, fumbled a pitch, and dropped a screen pass. The Tigers frustrated the Nittany Lions' offense and him.

After the game he took shots at Auburn running back Ronnie Brown, who rushed for 184 yards; the Auburn defensive players, whom he called soft; Paterno, whom he called inflexible; and Ganter, whose play calling he called too cute.

"When you look at my carries compared to his [Brown's], he had thirty-some carries," Johnson said. "You better have 100-some yards. If you get twenty carries against a good defense, there's no way in the world you're gonna go over 100. I don't think they shut me down.

"The last thing I would have done was try to pass. I would have tried to pound the ball and see what they would take. We didn't want to do that. We tried to trick them."

Despite his angst following the bowl game, Larry Johnson will be remembered as one of the greatest running backs in Penn State history. He came out of nowhere to become the Nittany Lions' first national leader in rushing and all-purpose yards, its first Walker Award winner and its seventh Maxwell Award winner.

"He was always on the verge [of being great]," Paterno said. "I used to tell him, 'Wait, wait, have a little patience.' When he finally got the feel of things, he was spectacular. Larry Johnson is a great football player, one of the greatest I have ever been around."

About the Author

Rich Scarcella has covered Penn State and college football for the Reading *Eagle* since 1989. He also has covered several other sports for the *Eagle* since 1986. He has received several national writing awards from The Associated Press Sports Editors and the Football Writers Association of America. He lives in Leesport, Pennsylvania, with his wife, Sandy, and their two sons, Eric and Joshua. This is his first book.